Guidance in Action:
Ideas and Innovations
for School Counselors

GUIDANCE IN ACTION: IDEAS AND INNOVATIONS FOR SCHOOL COUNSELORS

KENNETH U. GUTSCH
JOHN D. ALCORN

PARKER PUBLISHING COMPANY, INC.
West Nyack, N.Y.

© 1970 BY
PARKER PUBLISHING COMPANY, INC.
WEST NYACK, N.Y.

ALL RIGHTS RESERVED. NO PART OF THIS
BOOK MAY BE REPRODUCED IN ANY FORM
OR BY ANY MEANS, WITHOUT PERMISSION
IN WRITING FROM THE PUBLISHER.

LIBRARY OF CONGRESS
CATALOG CARD NUMBER: 78-92902

PRINTED IN THE UNITED STATES OF AMERICA
13-367912-8 B & P

A WORD FROM THE AUTHORS
ABOUT THIS BOOK . . .

For many years counselors have been exposed to programs of training which emphasize theory rather than practice. *Guidance in Action: Ideas and Innovations for School Counselors* shows the counselor how to go beyond theories. It is based on tested ideas and marked by innovations, a book with new thoughts for resolving many of the old and familiar guidance problems.

Through the tested ideas introduced within this book, counselors will have the opportunity to apply that special ingredient that makes guidance a reality rather than a concept. By presenting guidance in this way, counselors are provided not only with the potential for a more comprehensive and a more completely integrated program of services but with the understandings which are necessary for greater effectiveness in guidance.

Ultimately such an approach is designed to bring guidance to each student in the school and to provide for each student the opportunity to understand how he might benefit more fully from guidance services. When utilized to a vantage point, these ideas add a flavor of sophistication to guidance that may well serve to change the entire guidance picture within the school setting and to revitalize those areas that need strengthening.

Since the execution of an idea is never appropriate unless there is a rational basis for such action, this book does, whenever it seems essential, give limited attention to those theoretical concepts which precede the idea sequence. This will enable the reader to establish a basic frame of reference from which to work.

More specifically, the book introduces new ideas and analyzes speculative innovations which were born out of need and nurtured by years of guidance experience. It should bring the professional educator closer to his objectives through a greater involvement in, commitment to, and personal understanding of one of the most vital aspects of education.

Kenneth U. Gutsch
John D. Alcorn

CONTENTS

1. DEVELOPING A PERSONAL INVENTORY OF SKILLS AND OBJECTIVES **17**

    UNDERSTANDING INDIVIDUALS   19
    PERSON-TO-PERSON CONTACTS   19
    A SELF-TOLD STORY   21
    QUESTIONS AND ANSWERS   21
    LIFE: A DAY-TO-DAY ACCOUNT   21
    HOW DO OTHERS FEEL?   22
    A PERSONAL RATING   22
    JUST CHECKING   22
    A PERSONAL COMMENT   23
    VISITING THE HOME   23
    TESTING AND THE WORLD OF OBJECTIVITY   23
    WHERE DO WE START?   24
    TEST SELECTION AND RATIONALE   24
    ADMINISTERING AND SCORING   26
    GETTING THE FACULTY INVOLVED   27
    WHAT DOES IT ALL MEAN?   29
    WHEN A STUDENT BECOMES A CLIENT   29
    PUTTING IT IN THE RECORD   30

2. MASTERING EFFECTIVE EVALUATION TECHNIQUES: HOW TO COMMUNICATE RESULTS 35

BEGINNING THE EXPLORATION   36
LOOKING AT INTELLIGENCE OBJECTIVELY   39
UNDERSTANDING ACHIEVEMENT   40
CHECKING FOR APTITUDE   40
LOOKING AT CLIENT INTERESTS   41
OOPS! A PERSONALITY IS SHOWING   42
A FACE-TO-FACE CONTACT   43
BRINGING RESULTS TOGETHER   44
A CONFIDENTIAL REPORT   44

Preliminary Information · Intellectual Evaluation · Aptitude Evaluation · Interest Areas · Personal Inventory · Profile Summary

INFORMATION PERTAINING TO CONFIDENTIAL REPORT   53
IMPROVING THE COUNSELOR'S EFFICIENCY   53

How Important Is the Answer Sheet? · Finding Tests in a Hurry

3. EDUCATIONAL AND VOCATIONAL INFORMATION: KEEPING STUDENTS INFORMED   67

CLASSIFYING INFORMATION   67
AN INTERESTING INNOVATION   69
THE DISSEMINATION OF INFORMATION   70
IDEAS THAT SEEM TO HAVE MERIT   70
HOW TEACHERS MIGHT ASSIST   72

Gaining Teacher Cooperation · Developing an Occupational Monograph

LOOKING AT THE GROUP APPROACH   76

CONTENTS

4. USING A GROUP APPROACH EFFECTIVELY . . 79

    SOME DISTINGUISHING MARKS OF GROUPS 80
    IMPLEMENTING GROUP GUIDANCE 82
    THE TECHNIQUES INVOLVED 84
    THE PRINCIPLES INVOLVED 86
    VOCATIONAL-EDUCATIONAL ACTIVITIES 87
    GROUPS FORMED FOR PERSONAL EXPLORATION 88
    PRE-COLLEGE GUIDANCE 90

5. COUNSELING: IDEAS, INNOVATIONS, AND REALIZATIONS 93

    IDEAS 93

    The Problem of Impulsivity · The Problem of Depression · The Problem of Precounseling Orientation · Establishing a Precounseling Orientation Service

    INNOVATIONS 97

    Human Encounter: A Discerning Journey · What Precedes the Counseling Relationship? · Ideas Within the Counseling Relationship

    REALIZATIONS 102

    Theory and Practice in Action · The Case of Tony · Counseling and the Guidance Program · Role of the Counselor · Counseling Defined

6. WORKING WITH YOUNG STUDENTS 117

    SEX DIFFERENCES 117
    DISORDERS LEADING TO POOR READING 118

    Detecting Dyslexia · The Case of Frank

6. WORKING WITH YOUNG STUDENTS (*Continued*)

UNDERSTANDING SEPARATION ANXIETY 123
THE IMPACT OF ILLNESS ON PERFORMANCE 124
IDEAS ABOUT SHYNESS 125
DELINQUENCY: CAN WE PREDICT IT? 126
HELPING TEACHERS TO UNDERSTAND 127

7. PLACEMENT: A PATH TOWARD FULFILLMENT 135

A DUAL ROLE FOR PLACEMENT 135
PLACEMENT COUNSELING: PITFALLS AND ADMONITIONS 136
INVOLVING STUDENTS 137
A FUNCTIONAL APPROACH TO PLACEMENT 138

Educational Placement · Job Placement · Services to Employers · Services to Other Educational Institutions · Services to a School

COORDINATING YOUR EFFORTS WITH COMMUNITY AGENCIES 141

The State Employment Service · Private Employment Agencies · State Vocational Rehabilitation Service · Veterans Administration Counseling Program · Apprenticeship Program · Church Sponsored Guidance Programs · Selecting an Appropriate Agency

UNDERSTANDING THE EXPECTANCY GAP 145
CLOSING THE EXPECTANCY GAP 149

Providing Job Opportunity Information · Getting the Word to Employers

CONTACTING EMPLOYERS 158
WHAT TO EXPECT DURING THE EMPLOYMENT INTERVIEW 160

CONTENTS

7. **PLACEMENT: A PATH TOWARD FULFILLMENT** (*Continued*)

   USING DATA PROCESSING IN PLACEMENT 162
   IMPLEMENTING THE PLACEMENT SERVICE 162

8. **EVALUATING YOUR RESULTS: SOME INNOVATIONS THROUGH RESEARCH** . . . **165**

   WHY EVALUATE? 165
   CHARACTERISTICS OF A GOOD EVALUATION PROGRAM 166
   THREE KEY STEPS IN EVALUATION 167

   Defining Objectives · Developing "Yardsticks" · Employing Measures

   DEVELOPING THE EVALUATION MASTER PLAN 169
   GATHERING DATA FOR EVALUATION 169

   The Self-Study · The Case Study · The Survey · The Experimental Project · Analysis of Office Records

   THE FOLLOW-UP SERVICE 182

   Initiating the Follow-up Study · Implementing the Study

   PUTTING RESEARCH FINDINGS TO WORK 185

9. **IDEAS FOR ORGANIZING AND ADMINISTERING THE GUIDANCE PROGRAM** **187**

   STRUCTURING THE PROGRAM 188
   GETTING STAFF MEMBERS INVOLVED 193

   The Administrator's Responsibility · The Teacher's Responsibility · The Counselor's Responsibilities

9. IDEAS FOR ORGANIZING AND ADMINISTERING THE GUIDANCE PROGRAM (*Continued*)

TYPICAL PROBLEMS IN ORGANIZING A GUIDANCE PROGRAM   197
THE PRINCIPLE OF STAFF COMMUNICATION   199
GETTING PEOPLE INVOLVED   200
COMMUNICATING IDEAS THROUGH FOLKLORE   201

The Fountain · It's O.K. Son, Everybody Does It · Two Priests · One Solitary Life

INDEX   211

Guidance in Action: Ideas and Innovations for School Counselors

1

DEVELOPING A PERSONAL INVENTORY OF SKILLS AND OBJECTIVES

A number of years ago, some counselors hesitated to place any significant emphasis on test results because they were deeply concerned about the lack of objectivity in testing. Perhaps this attitude was magnified considerably by the influence of Rogerian concepts and the belief that once objective information about a student was secured, recorded, and interpreted, a situational event transpired which made it impossible for a counselor to free himself from the impressions created by this information. Then too, hesitancy and doubt may simply have been a reflection of feelings about tests that were generated by public distaste for specific types of test questions. Whatever the cause of these earlier attitudes, it now seems that the recent advent of electronic computers has done much to add a tone of sophistication to the area of testing and has thus created a refreshing attitude toward the utilization of test results. When supported by other information found within the confines of the Information Service, it now seems that test results will eventually provide understandings for students which were never before possible.

To explore the Individual Inventory and as a prelude to understanding the contributions that are possible through testing it seems extremely important to assist the reader in developing a frame of reference which introduces him to the Individual Inventory, to the nomenclature typically found associated with such an inventory, and to the ways in which the proper utilization of such an inventory lends itself to human understanding.

The cumulative record, by itself, serves as a chronological collection of material about an individual. Individual grades or test scores mean little by themselves but when collected over a period of time, form a pattern, the consistency of which we can seldom challenge. Whenever there is a sharp deviation or a gradual modification in this pattern, the counselor should immediately be alerted to a change. This chronological pattern, unlike any other source of data, not only telegraphs a change in the person's behavior but almost the exact period of time during which such change took place. Of considerable significance, of course, is the fact that when such a pattern is recorded from the elementary school on through high school, it gives the counselor the opportunity to search for such gradual changes as are normally reflected when a student suffers from a form of visual disorientation which permits him to function well with nonverbal materials but not so well with verbal materials. If this modification in performance is detected early enough, corrective measures can be taken which may be of greatest assistance to the student. The pattern is sometimes modified when the student has a traumatic experience such as a death in the family. Frequently, after such an experience his performance is at a low point and many times the only knowledge anyone has of his personal feelings is this modification in his performance pattern.

For the most part, an individual inventory service includes those data about the individual student considered important for his educational, vocational, and personal-social adjustment. One very important part of the individual inventory is the cumulative record. Although it is less broad and inclusive than the individual inventory it serves as a core from which the individual inventory derives written facts about the individual. It appears that the cumulative record best serves as a source of immediate data.

To paraphrase a statement Ruth Strang once made one might say that when properly kept the cumulative record is a reflection of the child's work, his interests, his personality, his home conditions, his recreational interests and many of the other factors that constitute a significant part of his existence. In its simplest form it becomes a compendium of a child's growth pattern while in its most sophisticated form it becomes a picture of the child's developmental pattern.[1]

UNDERSTANDING INDIVIDUALS

While there are many and varied concepts about what specific data should be obtained regarding the individual student, there is no doubt that all of the information should be recent, objective, and factual. Along with this consideration, there must also be some concern regarding the source of information itself, for it is from the source that the information derives great value. The three vital sources of information which one must consider when collecting information are: (1) the individual himself, (2) the individual's peer group, and (3) all others with whom the individual comes into contact. One way of viewing a structural pattern which reflects such a concept is expressed in Chart I.

Close observation of this chart will assist one to understand that it is necessary to employ a variety of techniques in an effort to elicit data which will supply an adequate background of information about the individual. Since these techniques, or intermediate sources of information as they are sometimes called, play such an important part in developing an understanding of the individual, perhaps it would be wise at this time to pursue a discussion of them.

PERSON-TO-PERSON CONTACTS

A very practical and effective method of collecting data is the interview. As may be seen in Chart I, interviews can be used to collect information about the individual not only from the student himself but also from peers, parents, relatives, and friends. The interview is generally recognized as a face-to-face

---

[1] Ruth Strang, *Every Teacher's Record* (Rev. Ed.; New York: Bureau of Publications, Teachers College, Columbia University, 1951), p. 10.

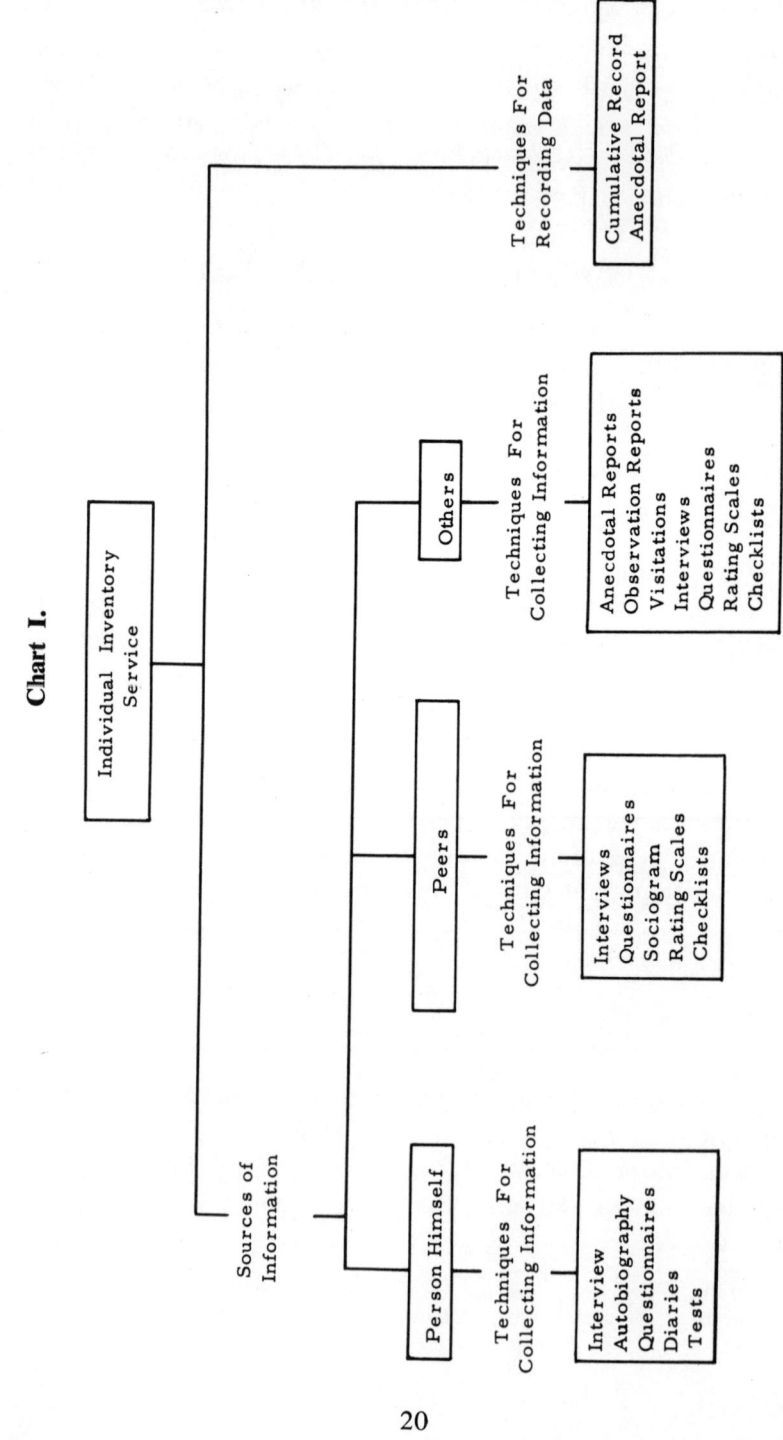

Chart I.

experience in which information getting, information giving, or acquaintanceship functions are of primary importance.

Although the interview is a most valuable and useful tool for collecting information about an individual it is not completely free from faults. The primary disadvantage in using the interview appears to stem from the fact that it is subject to misinterpretation on the part of the interviewer.

A SELF-TOLD STORY

An autobiography is usually thought of as an individual's life story presented in his own words and related to those things which he considers important. It is a tool which can be, and frequently is, used to assist counselors and others in gaining insight into a student's problems. If it is to be inclusive, it should follow a uniform format which remains flexible enough to include information which the student feels is important. The greatest disadvantage to the autobiography is that much is omitted through the individual's inability to respond frankly.

QUESTIONS AND ANSWERS

Perhaps one way of thinking of the questionnaire is to consider it a tool or device which permits its user to obtain attitudinal responses indicative of direction. This is to say that the questionnaire is capable of bringing out positive or negative facts which are related to the individual's background. Each questionnaire is constructed to fit the unique situation for which it is being used. The primary objective(s) of the questionnaire should always be explained to the individual answering the questions so that frank responses can be elicited. Its greatest disadvantage seems to stem from the fact that although direction of attitude is indicated, level of intensity of feeling is not included.

LIFE: A DAY-TO-DAY ACCOUNT

The diary is a continuous source or day-by-day account of a student's life. It is a fact-finding technique which is highly confidential. Both the autobiography and the diary can serve as a source of data often difficult to obtain from other sources. If at any time these techniques are used to project personality conflicts, it appears that they should be handled by staff members highly skilled in the use of projective techniques.

HOW DO OTHERS FEEL?

Sociograms are tools or devices which are commonly used to determine the interpersonal relationships within a group. Counselors may find the sociogram extremely useful in locating the status of each member within the group and, if necessary, providing for this member the opportunity to improve undesirable situations. It must be remembered that although this technique will give some indication of the class structure, it will not tell why these conditions exist nor how to resolve them.

All the questions on the sociometric device pertain to interpersonal relationships. As an example the instructor might say, "Today we are going to do committee work."

    (1) Name the person with whom you would best like to work ―――――――――――――.
    (2) Name your second choice ―――――――――.
    (3) Name your third choice ―――――――――.

The choices can be diagramed on a master sheet with first choices indicated by solid lines, second choices indicated by broken lines and third choices by dotted lines.

A PERSONAL RATING

A rating scale is frequently thought of as a device used to communicate impressions according to prescribed standards. It can be of considerable value when both the direction of feeling and intensity of feeling toward an attitude object are desired.

JUST CHECKING

The checklist is an instrument or device sometimes called a constant alternative. It is used primarily for making an accurate check of specific characteristics, qualities, abilities, or interests which an individual has.

Although quite useful as a time-saver, the disadvantage is that it gives direction of feeling without indicating intensity.

A PERSONAL COMMENT

The anecdotal record is a brief and descriptive account of incidents in the daily life of the student which are considered to be significant for his emotional and social adjustment. These reports should reflect not only the negative qualities of the individual but also the positive qualities. They should be brief and free from bias. A good record will contain three parts: (1) the incident, (2) an interpretation of exactly what happened, and (3) the recommendations for action relative to the incident.

VISITING THE HOME

The visitation is a direct method of obtaining information about the individual and is carried out when a counselor or teacher visits a student's home.

One of the disadvantages to be considered is that visitations are not only time-consuming but frequently pose a threat to the student.

TESTING AND THE WORLD OF OBJECTIVITY

Many of our modern day counselors are quite concerned with what students know when first entering the classroom and what their potentials are for learning. It is assumed that once assembled, information derived from testing situations can be used to assist the student in making a satisfactory adjustment in his role of everyday living. This approach, which recognizes individual differences and permits the individual the opportunity to be uniquely himself, reflects the guidance point of view. True, it isn't a new idea; Plato in his *Republic* recognized that individuals should perform tasks for which they were best suited and that education should be adapted to the capacities of each pupil; however, in our present-day educational system, this concept is considered necessary to the personal happiness of the individual as well as to his social usefulness.

WHERE DO WE START?

To explain the basis for a testing program and the philosophy underlying a program of this type appears quite simple, but to approach the program from a functional aspect is truly another thing. Perhaps one approach which may be considered of some value is to introduce the testing program through the cooperative efforts of a faculty committee. A committee of this kind could be organized to discover the needs of the students, the needs of the school, and the needs of the community as it is served by the school. With these needs as the objectives in mind, consultants can be brought in from the State Department of Education or from state universities or colleges. With consultants to serve as resource people as well as experts in methods of test selection, test administration, test scoring, test recording, and test reporting, the testing program takes on more meaning, and the information acquired from testing is better utilized.

TEST SELECTION AND RATIONALE

If, for any reason, the faculty committee chosen to initiate the testing program cannot get the assistance of a consultant, tests can be selected on the basis of answers to the following questions:
  1. Is the test valid? This is another way of asking whether or not the test measures what it purports to measure.
  2. Is the test reliable? This simply asks if the test measures whatever it measures with consistency.
  3. What are the norms? This question refers to the number of students that were used in an original test sample to establish a basis for the comparison of any person having a given characteristic with comparable individuals having the same characteristic.

The reason for testing with standardized tests seems to be four-fold: first, tests are a valuable means of securing information pertinent to the analysis of the individual and therefore serve to assist in counseling the individual; second, tests serve to assist in the identification of atypical students. This means that they help to identify the slow as well as the bright students; third, tests serve to assist teachers in evaluating their teaching methods; and fourth, tests serve the school administrators by assisting them to recognize the need for curriculum revision.

The standardized tests selected to perform these services are usually classified in the following manner:

1. *Achievement Tests*

    The primary design of the achievement test is to determine the degree to which the student has attained an understanding of concepts in a broad area of knowledge.

2. *Intelligence and Aptitude Tests*

    The intelligence test is most frequently considered a measurement of the student's potential or capacity for learning. The aptitude test is an expansion of this concept with the belief that there are several intelligences and that each is a reflection of a unique ability such as art, mechanical ability, music, etc.

3. *Interest Inventories*

    Although interest inventories are considered part of the testing program, they are not truly tests. They simply measure the individual's interests at any given time and become useful only when used with other guidance techniques.

4. *Adjustment Questionnaire*

    Personal adjustment questionnaires are not truly tests. They are inventories designed to assist the individual in developing a better self-concept. Their focus of attention usually deals with family problems, sexual problems, financial problems, and religious problems. It must be remembered that both the interest inventory and the adjustment questionnaire measure current attitudes and are therefore subject to change.

ADMINISTERING AND SCORING

Some administrators have felt that all testing should be done by a single examiner within the school system. The three major reasons for this point of view are:

1. The test is administered by a person who has carefully studied the testing procedure and is thoroughly familiar with the test to be administered.
2. The conditions of testing are much more likely to be uniform throughout the entire system.
3. The teachers have confidence that the test scores on record have not been invalidated by misadministration or mis-scoring.[2]

These advantages should be weighed against the following disadvantages of having all testing done by a single person:

1. The children are generally more relaxed with the classroom teachers than with the principal or an administrator.
2. The burden of work carried by a single administrator, giving tests in many different classrooms, is so great that little time is left for this trained person to aid in the important job of assisting teachers in the use and applications of the test results.
3. When testing is done by an administrator it is easy for the teachers to feel uninvolved and removed from the testing program.[3]

The procedure to be adopted for the administration of tests will vary from system to system and will depend largely on (1) the level of training of the teachers, (2) the amount of acceptance and understanding of the testing program, (3) the presence or absence of fear that one teacher's achievements will be compared with

---

[2] Kentucky State Department of Education, *Educational Bulletin: Guidance Services,* Vol. XXXIV, No. 9 (September, 1966), p. 31.
[3] *Ibid.*

those of another, and (4) whether or not there are specialized personnel.[4]

GETTING THE FACULTY INVOLVED

Once the tests have been selected by a guidance committee, a specific plan or systematic procedure such as an in-service training program might logically be employed to assist in the proper interpretation of test results. Following are some of the points upon which attention probably should be focused when training faculty members:

1. The purpose of each test must be explained to faculty members.
2. The teachers and counselors who are administering tests should take various sections of each test. This will assist them to gain a greater understanding of what the students must do and will provide for them an opportunity to avoid tests and inventories that contain offensive statements.
3. The knowledge acquired through self-application of the test should be transmitted to the students in an effort to create a favorable atmosphere by giving the students some idea of what they must do, how long it will take them, and how the results will be used to help them.
4. Adequate facilities should be available at all times and to all students.

A caution to be observed at this point is contained in R. H. Knapp's statement:

> Since tests are tools, they should always be used as a means to an end. That end, from the guidance point of view, is facilitating pupil adjustment according to pupil needs. Only those tests for which there is a need should be used. Indiscriminate testing without a purpose is poor practice.[5]

---
[4] *Ibid.*
[5] Robert H. Knapp, *Practical Guidance Methods* (New York: McGraw-Hill Book Company, Inc., 1953), p. 33.

Another consideration frequently confronting counselors is when to administer tests, the results of which might best assist classroom teachers. This appears to be a twofold problem that involves selecting the time of year to test and selecting the grade levels best suited to each area of testing. From all appearances it would seem that testing in the fall of the year permits the instructor to use the results as a means of understanding the student. Testing during the fall may even serve as a means of getting acquainted or establishing a favorable relationship with the student. On the other hand, to test in the spring may well serve as a disadvantage to the instructor since the students are, by this time, ready to advance to a higher grade level.

The grade level at which a test is administered is, of course, subject to the discretion of the test administrator, his knowledge of tests, the need he has for specific types of information at a given time, and his experience in the field of testing. Some people have opposed group testing at the first- and second-grade levels because students have not attained the psychomotor control necessary for paper and pencil testing. Others feel that students lack the necessary reading skill at such an early grade level. Viewing these opinions as worthy of consideration, it might be said that standardized group intelligence tests probably should be administered for the first time at grade three and given again at grades five, seven, and nine.

> The testing of intelligence may be supplemented by testing achievement at alternate grade levels if not every year ... for example, grades four, six, and eight. This procedure of alternating achievement and intelligence testing at different grade levels prevents the work of administering and scoring tests from falling on teachers at certain grade levels and involves all teachers in the process of pupil appraisal. As test results are recorded on the cumulative records it is easy to compare the results of the intelligence and achievement testing.[6]

---

[6] Kentucky State Department of Education, *Educational Bulletin: Guidance Services,* Vol. XXXIV, No. 9 (September, 1966), p. 33.

The Test Evaluation Checklist is included for convenience.* When counselors are asked to select tests, it will give them a specific frame of reference from which to work. Such checklists may also be used to assist teachers in evaluating tests being considered for classroom use.

After tests have been selected and properly administered, careful computation of the results and proper recording of them are paramount considerations.

WHAT DOES IT ALL MEAN?

Test interpretation requires training. Without some knowledge of the significance of testing and test interpretation, there is a tendency on the part of inadequately trained counselors to use the results as an absolute method for judging. Such indiscriminate action becomes quite serious when a counselor, for example, bases his judgment of a student's potential on a *single* I.Q. score.

With the proper training, counselors can become a definite aid to students by developing sophisticated understandings which will ultimately serve as a means of opening up new avenues of exploration to students. Through proper training, counselors will also learn to communicate test scores in a way which will not seriously upset or disturb parents. It must be remembered that testing can reveal the potentials and limitations of a student only —and this is the important point—only to the extent that the test is valid, reliable, properly administered, and the results are properly interpreted. Relative to this concept is the concept that the role of the guidance counselor or the faculty member is to assist in adjusting the school environment to the limitations and potentials which testing reveals.

WHEN A STUDENT BECOMES A CLIENT

When a student requests and receives counseling services, he becomes a special type student. As such, he is most appropriately

---

* Note: See end of chapter.

referred to as a client. This reference indicates that he has asked for and is receiving counseling services. It is a distinguishing mark which permits teachers, counselors and other professional people to understand immediately that he has applied for and is presently receiving a special type of assistance. Such understandings, although rather basic, make communications about this student easier and much more meaningful. It is for this reason that the authors have taken the liberty of referring to these special type students as clients throughout the book.

PUTTING IT IN THE RECORD

Once the information has been collected, some method of recording this data is necessary. The plan most commonly used in our present-day school system is the cumulative record. This record usually contains sufficient information to give a counselor a reasonably good understanding of what the student is like. However, in order to become completely cognizant of what a student is like, the counselor usually brings materials together in the form of a summary report.

A TEST EVALUATION CHECKLIST

General Information:

1. Name of Test _____

2. Author(s) _____

3. Name and Address of Publisher _____
   _____

4. Original Publication Date _____ Latest Revision _____

5. Purpose of Test _____
   _____

6. Levels and ranges (grades or ages) _____
   _____

7. Comparable forms available _____

A PERSONAL INVENTORY OF SKILLS AND OBJECTIVES 31

8. Price:

    Manual   _____
    Booklets   _____
    Answer Sheets _____
    Scoring Keys _____
    Other Services _____
    Specimen Sets _____

9. Specifically, what does test (or its subtests) purport to measure?

    a. _____
    b. _____
    c. _____
    d. _____
    e. _____

Validity:

   a. Does content appear to be reasonable for measuring trait(s) which test is supposed to measure?

                                        Yes ___ No ___

   b. What kinds of validity data are reported and what do the levels of validity appear to be? _____

   _____
   _____
   _____

   c. Have studies shown that the relationship between test results and criteria is sufficiently high for your purposes?

                                        Yes ___ No ___

   d. Has test been given favorable reviews in professional journals and Buros' *Mental Measurements Yearbook?*

                   Generally Yes ___   Generally No ___

   Comments: _____
   _____

Reliability:

	Level of Correlation	Number and Type of Subjects on which Check was made
Type Reliability Check		
Total Test: _____	_____	_____
Subtests: a. _____	_____	_____
b. _____	_____	_____
c. _____	_____	_____
d. _____	_____	_____
e. _____	_____	_____

Norms:

   a. Types of Normative Information reported: Age ___ Grade ___ Percentile ___ Stanines ___ Other _____

   b. Do test norms seem representative of the populations described? Yes ___ No ___

   c. Are norming populations similar enough to your population to allow comparability? Yes ___ No ___

Usability:

   a. Time required to give test: Actual working time ___ min. Estimated Administration time ___ min.

   b. Can test be administered to groups as well as to individuals? Yes ___ No ___

   c. Does test require special equipment or apparatus other than paper and pencil? Yes ___ No ___
If so, what? _____

   d. Special training required for administration _____

   e. Scoring:

      (1) Is test objectively scored? Yes ___ No ___

(2) Is scoring easy to understand?
Yes ___ No ___

f. Do testing materials facilitate interpretation?
Yes ___ No ___

g. Readability: Good ___ Fair ___ Poor ___

h. Overall recommendation for selection and use of test:

Date _____   Reviewed by _____

2

MASTERING EFFECTIVE EVALUATION TECHNIQUES: HOW TO COMMUNICATE RESULTS

Although much attention has been focused on testing and interviewing, little has been written on the subject of guidance reporting, i.e., reporting to parents, teachers, administrators and others those objective results obtained through testing. Such reporting is, in itself, a unique challenge that requires an ability to bring together materials which are pertinent to an objective understanding of the student and to report the findings of such materials in a way which is not only ethical but which permits the student to understand himself and the world in which he exists. If the student is to grow—that is, if he is to go beyond his status quo—then it seems essential that he understand where he is, what he is like, where he can go in terms of his potential for growth, and what obstacles or restrictions he might encounter as he journeys from where he is to where he wants to go. Basically, the essence of such an idea has a great deal to do with goal orientation. What is the student like? Can we assist him to understand his goals in terms of his past accomplishments and his present potentials? Such an understanding of the student takes into account his total scholastic performance, his environmental conditions, his potential for growth, his immediate ability to think intelligently when working with both verbal and nonverbal materials, his ability to function organically (to function without visual, hearing or other organic disabilities) and his ability to adapt to situations which involve personal contacts.

BEGINNING THE EXPLORATION

To undertake an objective study of a student requires a systematic pattern of testing, interviewing, profiling, and reporting. Perhaps the first step in such a pattern is the Intake Interview. It is at this point of initial contact with the counselor that the student becomes a client, i.e., a special type student who has requested and is now receiving counseling services. Because the Intake Interview represents the initial contact with the client, it seems extremely important and should be designed with some structuring. The Personal Data Sheets included in this chapter reflect some of the information that might normally be sought through the utilization of an Intake Interview (see Personal Data Sheet Form). Once this information is obtained, the counselor is able to include in his confidential report a section which might most appropriately be labeled Preliminary Information. When the client's confidential report is finally completed and placed in the hands of parents or professional people who use this information to assist and understand him, the section on Preliminary Information will serve to clarify understandings relative to the client's family life, his environment, his health, and his present ability to achieve scholastically. Such information as might normally be found in this section may, in most instances, be obtained from the client, from his parents, from his medical doctor, and/or from his guardian.

PERSONAL DATA SHEET

Completion of the information requested on this form will enable your counselor to be of greater assistance to you.

Name _____ Date _____
School or college _____ Class _____
Home address _____
Present address _____

Sex ___ Date of birth _____ Age ___ Place of birth _____
Married ___ Single ___ Separated ___ Divorced ___ Widowed ___

Indicate all members of your family, including parents, husband or wife, children, brothers and sisters.

Relationship	Age	Occupation (be specific)	Marital Status	Years of Education
_____	_____	_____	_____	_____
_____	_____	_____	_____	_____
_____	_____	_____	_____	_____
_____	_____	_____	_____	_____

EDUCATION:

	Name of School	Last Grade Completed	Date of Completion
Elementary	_____	_____	_____
High School or Vocational	_____	_____	_____
College or University	_____	_____	_____
Professional or Other	_____	_____	_____

High School Grades Eng. ___ Math. ___ Soc. Sci. ___
                                         Nat. Sci. ___

What subjects do you like best? _____ least? _____
In what activities or organizations have you taken part?
High School _____
Held Office In _____
College _____
Held Office In _____
My major is _____ I chose this field because _____

WORK EXPERIENCE:

Part-time work for which you were paid:

Job	Employer	Dates
_____	_____	_____
_____	_____	_____

Full-time work:

_____	_____	_____
_____	_____	_____

38 EVALUATION TECHNIQUES: HOW TO COMMUNICATE RESULTS

List the careers which you have considered seriously and those which appeal to you most now:

Occupation   *Reason for interest in the occupation*
_____   _____
_____   _____

Hobbies or interests you may have: _____
_____

CASE HISTORY:
Weight _____ Height _____ Eyes (color) _____ Glasses _____
Disease Experience: Has client experienced any difficulty with any of the following: (Please explain any checks in the space provided below. If more space is needed, use additional page.)

  Discipline _____
  Sleeping _____
  Eating _____
  Language _____
  Motor Movement _____
  Reactions to Peers _____
  Reactions to Adults _____
  Other: _____

Explanation: _____
_____
_____
_____
_____

Perhaps as a second step in working with a client some effort should be made to staff the case; that is, a staffing or case conference should take place with faculty members who are assisting with the guidance program or who are members of the guidance staff. This will permit the counselor an opportunity to outline a series of tests and inventories which will hopefully serve as the most expedient measures available in terms of goal orientation. Although these tests may be introduced in different sequences, the present sequence is used as an illustration of what might be done.

LOOKING AT INTELLIGENCE OBJECTIVELY

Since experience indicates that Science Research Associates (SRA) verbal and nonverbal tests will do much to establish a basic frame of reference from which the counselor can work, these tests are sometimes administered during the first meetings with the client. When both the SRA verbal and nonverbal tests are administered during comparable periods of time, i.e., during the same day, the results of such tests will not only indicate the client's verbal and nonverbal potential but will permit a fairly comprehensive evaluation of his visual proficiency. This is to say that if a person does not perform well on either the SRA verbal or the SRA nonverbal test of intelligence, a review of his total response pattern on these tests may be in order. Assuming that he is not performing at a low level because of ill health, such a review may indicate that in both verbal and nonverbal tests his eye movement was extremely slow and that he experiences a problem related to vision rather than to intelligence. One method which can be used to explore the response repertoire for such mistakes is to mark response items that were answered during the time allotted for administration of these SRA tests and then to administer the remaining test items in an untimed situation. If the client's score is noticeably affected by such a technique, results will not only reflect the client's potential for scoring higher on factors of intelligence which are presented in an untimed situation, but will also indicate whether or not the client should be referred for a series of visual tests in an effort to further define his difficulty.

If the client does well on the nonverbal test but poorly on the verbal test, i.e., a difference of twelve or more points, this may indicate that he is experiencing some difficulty with words. It may actually be an indication of such problems as are sometimes encountered when working with dyslexics. Another possible cause for a broad differentiation in scores on these two tests might be attributed to such visual difficulties as are reflected by persons who experience problems with fusion.

If the client does well on the verbal test and poorly on the nonverbal test, such results may indicate the need for further exploration of the client's personality characteristics with special attention focused on impulsivity.

UNDERSTANDING ACHIEVEMENT

As a natural adjunct to intelligence testing, achievement testing is of considerable importance. It now appears that without some knowledge of the client's ability to achieve, little understanding can be gained relative to his academic aspirations and his consistency of performance within the idiom of academic pursuit.

If a client performs at an academic level which exceeds his expectations as reflected by standardized achievement test scores, then it may be that some bias has been created through his relations with those who assign grades. It is also possible that teachers are consistent in their grading but that their grading is higher in terms of local norms than it would be if they were forced to use national norms. Another possibility is that the student experienced some personal difficulty when taking the standardized tests and that his standardized achievement test scores are simply a reflection of his sensitivity to other problems.

Although many such explanations seem valid, they are highly speculative until additional information is obtained. It is for this reason that reports should never be introduced prematurely or without substantiating data. Remember that this chapter is not designed to scrutinize all possible evaluative approaches but rather to alert those individuals who have minimal test experience to some of the possible ways of using test results.

CHECKING FOR APTITUDE

Of considerable significance to the client's understanding of "self" is his ability to understand his potential. It is true that his ability to utilize what he has in terms of objectives is a quality characteristic which takes priority, but this priority comes only after there is reasonable evidence to indicate that the client actually has the necessary potential to transcend his status quo.

As another means to understanding human development, aptitude testing is perhaps one of the more sophisticated approaches. Anyone who works with tests should be cognizant of the fact that aptitude indicates potential and does not suggest that a person is capable of that potential unless he makes a personal effort in an area which lends itself well to his potential. When considering such potential, it is always good to consider it in terms of past performance records. If such performance records seem to indicate difficulty in academic adaptation, then it seems obvious that the client must understand his potential for growth in terms of presently existing conditions and limitations. Why a person has the potential to work toward specific goals but does not elect to do so will perhaps be better understood in terms of interests and aspirations.

LOOKING AT CLIENT INTERESTS

Another step toward understanding human development concerns itself with an exploration of interests. If the client experiences cultural encapsulation, it will perhaps be difficult for him to look at interest areas with any degree of realism. The Kuder Preference Record Vocational Interest Form permits the client to explore broad interest patterns. Through an exploration of this nature, the counselor can combine interest areas with such factors as achievement, intelligence, aptitude and personality—a procedure which ultimately helps to narrow the field of vocational choice.

Counselors should be alerted to the fact that in at least some instances vocational interests are more a reflection of curiosity or emotions than they are of actual interests. For example, D. B. Feather [1] found that a group of students defined by results on the MMPI as maladjusted scored higher on the artistic, literary, and musical scales of the Kuder. Although this could be an indication of real interest, it seems that it could also be a reflec-

---

[1] Don B. Feather, "The Relation of Personality Maladjustments of 503 University of Michigan Students to Their Occupational Interests," *Journal of Social Psychology*, Vol. XXXII (August, 1950), pp. 71–78.

tion of the need for escape—a need for escape which becomes manifest in an interest pattern that complements the type of expression that creative artists have. This does not mean that those who score high in these three areas are, of necessity, in need of personal psychological assistance but rather that a group of high scores in these areas may merit further consideration if inventory results are to be used to assist the client to understand himself and the world in which he lives.

Unfortunately, it is difficult to determine whether or not a client has a real interest in a vocational area until he has been introduced to occupational briefs and other pertinent materials related to that area. Such an attempt to explore information is introduced only after a complete profile of test and inventory results has been compiled in a meaningful way. Once this has been done, it is possible to readminister the Kuder in an effort to refine the client's understanding of his true interests. It should be remembered as one works with interest areas that a high score in an area does not constitute an ability in that area but is simply an expression of interest.

OOPS! A PERSONALITY IS SHOWING

Although much has been done to discourage the use of personality inventories within the confines of our public school settings, it now seems that a confidential summary report which gave no consideration to such characteristics would be without practical value to the client. Personality inventories are designed to explore, in depth, those feelings and attitudes a client has about significant ideas, events, and other experiences in his life and how he acts or reacts to these experiences. These inventories are designed to assist an individual in understanding how he interacts personally and socially in terms of how others of his age group interact. Such information seems extremely important for it serves as the point omega of understanding in the area of counseling. If, through an exploration of personality characteristics, it is found that the client enjoys working with groups but that in his work he will be authoritative and demanding, such information can be of much assistance to the client who seeks to become integrated—the person who seeks to adapt to the world of work by enjoying a state of harmony within the confines of his job.

When counseling with students who desire to enter the area of vocational exploration, personality characteristics become of vital importance. Actually, it is only through feelings of stability and security that clients are capable of making logical, rational, and valid occupational choices. As these personality characteristics are considered along with achievement, intelligence, aptitude, and interest, much can be done to narrow the choice field—to assist the individual to make choices in terms of his own abilities and capabilities.

A FACE-TO-FACE CONTACT

Interviews serve as a means of making an initial contact with a client and assist the counselor to maintain a vigilance relative to this contact. The Intake Interview serves as the first contact with the client and is perhaps of more importance in counseling than any other, for it assists the client to establish a frame of reference relative to the services he is now requesting. It provides for the client some understanding about counseling experiences and in so doing creates for him a feeling of whether or not such services will be threatening—whether or not these are services he actually needs, and what might be expected as a direct result of such services. The sequence of interviews conducted after the Intake Interview serves to seal the bond of unity between the counselor and the client. These interviews presumably should provide a climate which permits the client sufficient latitude to explore those things in his life which he feels are extremely important but which he sometimes hesitates to talk about when he is with people other than the counselor. It is through this climate of free expression that the client is permitted to grow and is encouraged to develop an attitude which will assist him in committing himself to responsibilities designed to benefit both himself and the society in which he exists.

BRINGING RESULTS TOGETHER

Perhaps one of the most difficult problems relative to reporting is bringing data together in a way which will not create a threat to the client nor a feeling of embarrassment for his parents. In an effort to create such a climate, it now appears that considerable attention will have to be given to semantics. This is simply to say that when working with tests or inventories in which such terms as "anxiety" are used, reports to parents, teachers, and administrators are perhaps best facilitated by changing the terms. In this particular case the term anxiety can be changed to anxiousness. Since a professional person will understand the term anxiousness as readily as he does anxiety the report has not lost any of its value. Yet, for the parents and for the client the term anxiousness seems much less threatening.

A small consideration such as this makes reporting more practical since clients who are threatened by introductory statements in a report seldom, if ever, gain sufficient composure to understand the remaining parts of the report.

Much of what goes into a final report—the content of the report—must be considered in terms of all those individuals for whom the report is written. Since clients, teachers, administrators, parents, medical doctors, psychiatrists, clinical psychologists, reading experts, and speech and hearing experts may be interested in such a report and since some of these individuals do not understand test results, one approach to reporting involves introducing brief descriptions of the tests and inventories.

Following is a confidential report which serves as an example of one approach to what can be done through the utilization of a limited amount of materials.

A CONFIDENTIAL REPORT

Tests Administered

Name: Mr. X
Age: 18

1. Otis Quick-Scoring Mental Abilities Test

Status: High School Senior
Source of Referral: Teacher
Purpose: Vocational and
    Educational Exploration

2. Raven Progressive Matrices
3. SRA Verbal Test
4. SRA Non-Verbal Test
5. General Aptitude Test Battery
6. Kuder Preference Record Personal
7. Kuder Preference Record Vocational
8. How Well Do You Know Yourself *

Preliminary Information

The client is a white male, 18 years of age and a senior at Central High School in Jackson, Mississippi. He has no apparent physical defects.

The client was given a battery of tests and inventories designed to facilitate educational planning and vocational choice.

Prior to taking this battery of tests, the client indicated that he had contacted several colleges in preparation for his future academic commitments. During his first contacts with the counselor, the client expressed an interest in becoming an architect, forest ranger, or park ranger.

Intellectual Evaluation

An intellectual evaluation was made by administering the following instruments: The Otis Quick-Scoring Mental Abilities Test, the Raven Progressive Matrices, the SRA Verbal Test, the SRA Non-Verbal Test, and the GATB Factor G.

The Otis Quick-Scoring Mental Ability Test. This instrument has as its stated purpose the measuring of "thinking power or the degree of maturity of the mind."

---

* Permission to use the materials herein relative to this instrument has been granted by Executive Analysis Corp., 76 Beaver St., New York.

The Raven Progressive Matrices. This instrument reflects a person's capacity to apprehend meaningless figures presented for observation, see the relation between them, and conceive the nature of the figure completing each system of relations presented, and by so doing, develop a systematic method of reasoning. The scale consists of sixty problems divided into five sets of twelve. In each set the first problem is as nearly as possible, self-evident. The problems which follow become progressively more difficult. The five sets provide five opportunities for grasping the method and five progressive assessments of a person's capacity for intellectual activity. A person's total score provides an index of his intellectual capacity, whatever his nationality or education. This test is nonverbal and untimed.

The SRA Verbal Test. This test has been developed through many years of research to furnish an objective index of student intelligence.

The SRA Non-Verbal Test. This test uses items proved by research to test ability to reason out differences in pictured objects. No reading is required. Research has shown that recognition of differences is basic to learning.

Results of the Otis Quick-Scoring Mental Ability Test and the SRA Non-Verbal Test indicate that the client's scores were in the superior range. His scores on the Raven Progressive Matrices and the SRA Verbal Test were in the above average range. His score on the General Aptitude Test Battery (G) tends to confirm this classification.

Aptitude Evaluation

General Aptitude Test Battery. The purpose of the General Aptitude Test Battery is to help relate the potential abilities that the client possesses to aptitudes as required for each of 36 job families.

The client's scores in rank order are:

Spatial Aptitude	130
G Factor	Superior
Form Perception	115

Verbal Aptitude   106
Numerical Aptitude   95
Clerical Perception   87

According to the results of this test, it appears that the client possesses aptitudes required for each of 27 of the 36 job families developed by the United States Employment Service. It appears that these areas would be worthy of exploration by the client.

It should be remembered that this laboratory does not give the Finger Dexterity Test (F) nor the Manual Dexterity Test (M). This means that there are possibly 19 additional aptitude patterns for which the client might be suited.

Interest Areas

The Kuder Preference Record—Vocational. This is a device for indicating vocational interests. This instrument was used in an attempt to discover the client's major interest areas. A score which falls above the 75th percentile is interpreted as a significant interest. A score which falls below the 25th percentile is considered to indicate a lack of interest. Scores ranging from the 26th percentile to the 74th percentile are considered of normal or average interest and cannót be regarded with so much confidence.

The client's interests in rank order are:

Persuasive   94th percentile
Artistic   82nd percentile
Scientific   65th percentile
Mechanical   64th percentile
Computational   63rd percentile
Clerical   56th percentile
Music   48th percentile
Outdoor   32nd percentile
Literary   12th percentile
Social Service   9th percentile

The Kuder Preference Record—Personal. This inventory tends to show the kind of relations preferred with other people and the situations in which the client prefers to work.

The client's interests in rank order are:

Avoiding Conflict 96th percentile
Group Activity 60th percentile
Dealing with Ideas 49th percentile
Stable Situations 41st percentile
Directing Others 20th percentile

Personal Inventory

How Well Do You Know Yourself. This inventory provides scores which are specifically designed to aid or facilitate the study and assessment of the individual examinee by such specialists as guidance workers, counselors, and personnel officers. The seventeen scores represent primary factors. The description or meaning of each scale score is given below. It is in terms of these decriptions rather than in terms of dictionary definitions of the one-word titles that the scores for each scale are to be interpreted. The 50th percentile is considered about average. The client's scores are as follows:

Irritability (80th percentile). A tendency to become annoyed or upset when one feels thwarted or frustrated by people or conditions.

Practicality (41st percentile). A tendency to think about and to cope with the environment in relation to practical or utilitarian needs.

Punctuality (31st percentile). A tendency toward promptness or concern about timeliness or punctuality in meeting schedules and commitments as opposed to tardiness, dilatoriness.

Novelty-loving (38th percentile). A tendency to like situations involving new decisions, plans, goals or new ways of doing things in contradistinction to mere variety without novelty.

Vocational Assurance (12th percentile). A tendency to feel capable of achieving the financial or occupational rewards which one needs or desires.

Cooperativeness (41st percentile). A tendency to identify oneself with and work with others to achieve common goals.

Ambitiousness (53rd percentile). A tendency to desire and to strive for personal preferment or advancement in the sense of seeking marks of success or prestige, such as fame, honor, money, and influence.

Hypercriticalness (57th percentile). A tendency toward noticing and pointing out the faults, mistakes or shortcomings of others as well as a tendency to direct attention to and to overemphasize these faults.

Dejection (81st percentile). A tendency to feel low-spirited, unhappy, depressed, and/or disheartened.

General Morale (9th percentile). A general tendency to feel optimistic, hopeful or satisfied with respect to both the world at large and one's present and future status in it.

Persistence (29th percentile). A tendency to continue against opposing forces, either outside or within oneself.

Nervousness (21st percentile). A tendency to feel jumpy, tense, restless, or unable to relax, sometimes manifested by fidgeting and exhibiting nervous habits such as tics.

Seriousness (15th percentile). A tendency to assume an attitude of earnestness or to exhibit feelings of personal responsibility toward one's work or environment.

Submissiveness (35th percentile). A tendency to comply with what others expect one to do and to submit to domination rather than to resist it.

Dynamism (36th percentile). A tendency to feel lively, active, or energetic with a sense of vigorous physical well-being.

Emotional Control (20th percentile). A tendency to inhibit or restrain socially disapproved emotional reactions, such as controlling one's temper in disagreeable situations or remaining calm when others become upset.

Profile Summary

Within the confines of the information now available relative to the client, it appears that he is a person of above average to superior intelligence with his scores on the upper end of the average continuum. (Otis, Ravens, SRA, and GATB–Factor G). This high intellectual ability combined with high aptitude scores (GATB), indicates that the client has the potential to perform well in many areas. Specifically, the client appears to have those aptitudes which lend themselves well to performance in twenty-seven of the occupational patterns developed by the United States Employment Service.

It should be remembered that aptitude is a term which in itself or in its simplest form indicates potential. It does not, however, indicate success will come without effort and appropriate adaptation.

It must also be remembered that aptitude and interest are not identical and that a person may have an aptitude or potential for an area without possessing any immediate interest in the area. Conversely, it is also true that a person may have an interest in an area without possessing an aptitude for the area.

The client indicates an interest in work areas that include persuasive and artistic traits (Kuder Preference Record—Vocational). Possible areas for exploration might include:

Persuasive—Professional
0–06 Author, Editor, Reporter
0–06 Public Relations Worker
0–19 Sales Engineer
0–22 Lawyer, Judge
0–39 Personnel and Employment Manager

Artistic—Professional
0–02 Actor
0–03 Architect
0–04 Artist, Sculptor, Teacher of Art
0–32 Occupational Therapist
0–39 Curator of an Art Gallery

Combinations of these interest areas may provide the following areas for exploration:

Persuasive—Artistic (*Professional*)
0–04 Cartoonist
0–56 Photographer (Commercial)

0-72 Store Manager (flowers, gifts, art goods, antiques)

To narrow the field of selection further, the client might note that inventory results (Kuder Preference Record—Personal) indicate a significant interest in situations in which he would avoid conflict with others and a lack of interest in directing others. The client appears to like smooth, pleasant social situations and is willing to make considerable effort to preserve friendly relations. It appears that he may feel somewhat less comfortable in situations which influence the thoughts and activities of other people. Perhaps personal counseling might be of some service in his development of greater assertiveness. If he would like to receive such services, it is possible that his high school counselor can continue in this area.

It should be noted that professional areas only have been listed previously and should be considered only if the client goes to college. Other work areas of interest in nonprofessional vocations are listed here. Again, it must be remembered that this is a partial listing and that many of these areas require post high school training.

Persuasive Semi-Professional
0-69 Radio Announcer

Persuasive—Artistic
Sales and Kindred
1-51 Auctioneer (art goods)
1-75 Salesperson (decorative household accessories, floor coverings, flowers, jewelry)
1-87 Advertising Salesman
1-87 Salesman of Art Goods

Artistic Semi-Professional
0-43 Decorator and Window Dresser
0-44 Commercial Artist
0-46 Designer
0-56 Draftsman
0-56 Photographer
0-66 Taxidermist

Inventory results (How Well Do You Know Yourself) indicate that the client appears to function toward the lower end of the continuum in the areas of vocational assurance, general morale, nervousness, seriousness and emotional control, and above average in the areas of irritability and dejection. This may indicate that at times the client has a tendency to feel annoyed, and perhaps downcast. Since it seems natural that the client may be concerned about his vocational future it is possible that some of the feelings he reflects are related to goal orientation. That is to say, he feels some concern relative to both the world at large and his present and future status in it. The client's below average acedemic performance may be a reflection of his lack of goal orientation, his inability to think seriously about his future at this time, his feelings of dejection, and his inability to tolerate certain annoying and/or frustrating situations with which he seems to be confronted. Such considerations as he might give these characteristics and feelings at this time may be instrumental to his academic progress in high school and later in college, if he attends college.

In review, the client appears to be a person of above average to superior ability with the potential to perform well in college if he adapts well to his present academic situation. Although the client has stated an interest in the area of architecture, it must be remembered that his previous academic performance in the area of mathematics cannot go without consideration. It now seems that he must make some effort to overcome his deficiency in the area of mathematics or that he must continue to explore avenues of vocational growth which are more appropriate to his past performance—i.e., those areas of vocational exploration which are commensurate with his capabilities, interests, and previous performance record.

Since the final decision will ultimately rest with the client, our guidance services remain open to him for purposes of exploration through the utilization of occupational briefs, abstracts, monographs, and books. We hope that he will feel free to use this service at his convenience.

INFORMATION PERTAINING TO CONFIDENTIAL REPORT

After the Confidential Report has been prepared the client or his guardian is given a final copy and is asked to sign a release so that other professional people may utilize this information. If the client, his parents, or his guardian do not want such information released, the counselor has an ethical obligation to keep the information confidential unless it is subpoenaed by a court order.

Release Form

Date _____

I have read the information in this report and am willing to have it released for use by such *professional persons* as may be needed.

_____ _____
Counselor   Client, Parent or Guardian

IMPROVING THE COUNSELOR'S EFFICIENCY

How Important Is the Answer Sheet?

For those who have minimal budgets and cannot afford to develop a sophisticated program of testing, the following ideas may be helpful:

Idea I: Examine the answer sheet and watch for students who respond impulsively. Their response pattern is frequently characterized by a uniquely consistent pattern of incorrect responses after the student has reached a certain item. To examine an IBM scoring sheet that was completed by such a person sometimes gives one the impression that after the student reached a specific test item, he simply responded to the remaining items irrationally.

His impulsivity appears to be marked both by the consistency of his incorrect response pattern and by his lack of deviation in selecting alternative response items. That is to say that once his impulsivity is cued, he may frequently respond without making any effort to change to another alternative response. On an IBM scoring sheet the impulsive person will, in at least some instances, have a straight-line pattern of incorrect responses after reaching the item which cued his impulsivity.

Idea II: Examine the answer sheet and watch for students who appear to be anxious. Their response pattern vacillates considerably. When they have recorded their responses on IBM answer sheets, it seems obvious from their response patterns that they frequently omit items which are on the easy end of the test item continuum. It also seems obvious that they frequently erase responses and select other responses. When both characteristics are reflected with a definite consistency throughout the response pattern, we have found the student to be anxious.

Idea III: Review the total response pattern to determine Total Test Items (TTI), Total Responses Attempted (TRA), Total Responses Correct (TRC), and the percent of accuracy relative to the total number of responses. The purpose of this approach is, of course, to determine whether or not students may be experiencing visual difficulties. Since many schools are not equipped to conduct complete and thorough visual examinations, it seems imperative to use every conceivable method to assist in developing a better understanding of students. By using this technique the counselor can gain much insight into what must be done to assist the student to transcend his status quo.

For example, if on the Otis (Gamma) a student who was 18 years old had a raw score of 42, this raw score would convert to an I.Q. of 100. If this person attempted no more than 42 items out of the total of 80, then his accuracy would be 100 percent. This I.Q. of 100 would not mean the same thing as the same I.Q. score made by a student of the same age who attempted 80 items but had only 42 correct. Although both had the same raw score and the same I.Q., the first case must be explored further to determine whether or not the client is experiencing some visual problem.

Finding Tests in a Hurry

For those counselors who experience difficulty when searching for inventories and tests which are appropriate for specific grade levels, the Gutsch-Alcorn Test Scanner (GATS), Figure 2–1, may be of some assistance. The list of publishers found at the end of this chapter corresponds with the publisher's code found on the GATS and may be of some help to those who want to purchase tests or secure more information about these tests. To use the GATS effectively the reader has only to find the tests and inventories which seem to lend themselves well to his needs. All tests and inventories are profiled relative to grade levels which are listed as most appropriate by the publishers. To get additional information about these inventories and tests, simply take the publisher's code number from the GATS and find the number on the list of publishers which corresponds with this code number.

GATS

GUTSCH-ALCORN TEST SCANNER

TEST	*PUBLISHER'S CODE NO.	K-3	4	5	6	7	8	9	10	11	12	College
ACHIEVEMENT												
Army General Classification Test	20											
California Achievement Test Battery	4											
College Qualification Test	18											
Engle Psychology Test	11											
Essential High School Content Battery	23											
General Achievement Test	22											
Iowa High School Content Examination	3											
Iowa Test of Educational Development	20											
Metropolitan Achievement Battery	23											
Progressive Achievement Test	4											
SRA Achievement Series	20											
Stanford Achievement Battery	11											
Wide Range Achievement Test	13											
ACHIEVEMENT (DIAGNOSTIC)												
100 Problem Arithmetic Test	23											

*See page 64 for list of code numbers and corresponding publishing companies and addresses.

TEST	*PUBLISHER'S CODE NO.	GRADE LEVEL
		K-3, 4, 5, 6, 7, 8, 9, 10, 11, 12, College
SRA Basic Skills in Arithmetic Test	20	
Understanding the Meanings in Arithmetic	20	
Barrett English	23	
Michigan Vocabulary Test	23	
ADJUSTMENT INVENTORIES		
Bell Adjustment Inventory	6	
College Inventory of Academic Adjustment	21	
Heston Personal Adjustment Inventory	23	
APTITUDE TESTS		
Detroit Test of Learning Aptitudes	2	
Differential Aptitude Test	18	
Academic Promise Test	18	
Aptitude Test for Occupations	4	
ACE Psychological Examination	7	
Flanagan Aptitude Classification Test	20	

*See page 64 for list of code numbers and corresponding publishing companies and addresses.

Figure 2–1 (continued).

TEST	*PUBLISHER'S CODE NO.	GRADE LEVEL										
		K-3	4	5	6	7	8	9	10	11	12	College
Macquarrie Test of Mechanical Ability	4											
Mechanical Comprehension Test	18											
Minnesota Clerical Test	18											
Minnesota Paper Form Board Test	18											
Multiple Aptitude Test	4											
SRA Clerical Aptitude Test	20											
SRA Mechanical Aptitude	20											
Turse Clerical Aptitude	23											
Turse Shorthand Aptitude Test	11											
INTELLIGENCE TESTS												
California Tests of Mental Maturity	4											
Culture Fair IQ Scale I	14											
Test of "g" Culture Fair	14											
Davis Elles Test of General Intelligence	23											
Full Range Picture Vocabulary Test	17											
Henmon-Nelson	12											
Holzinger Crowder Uni-Factor	11											
Kuhlman-Anderson Test	16											
Otis Quick Scoring Mental Ability Test	11											

*See page 64 for list of code numbers and corresponding publishing companies and addresses.

Figure 2–1 (continued).

TEST	*PUBLISHER'S CODE NO.	K-3	4	5	6	7	8	9	10	11	12	College
Pinter Cunningham General Ability	11											
SRA Primary Mental Abilities	20											
SRA Test of Educational Ability	20											
SRA Test of General Ability	20											
SRA Verbal and Non-Verbal	20											
Terman-McNemar Test of Mental Ability	23											
Slosson Intelligence Test	24											
Cooperative Primary Tests												
INTEREST INVENTORIES												
General Interest Survey	20											
Gordon Occupational Check List	11											
Kuder Vocational	20											
Occupational Interest Inventory	4											
How Well Do You Know Your Interests	10											
Strong Vocational Interest Blank for Men	6											
Strong Vocational Interest Blank for Women	6											

*See page 64 for list of code numbers and corresponding publishing companies and addresses.

Figure 2–1 (continued).

TEST	*PUBLISHER'S CODE NO.	GRADE LEVEL										
		K-3	4	5	6	7	8	9	10	11	12	College

PERSONALITY

Test	Code
ACE Psychological Examination	1
Behavior Preference Record	4
Bernreuter-Personality Inventory	21
Childrens Personality Questionnaire	14
California Test of Personality	4
How Well Do You Know Yourself	10
Gordon Personal Profile and Personal Inventory	11
K-D Proneness Check List (Revised)	23
Kuder Personal	20
Mooney Problem Check List	18
Minnesota Counseling Inventory	18
Motivation Analysis Test	14
Neuroticism Scale Questionnaire	14
Sixteen Personality Factor Questionnaire	14

*See page 64 for list of code numbers and corresponding publishing companies and addresses.

Figure 2-1 (continued).

TEST	*PUBLISHER'S CODE NO.	K-3	4	5	6	7	8	9	10	11	12	College
SRA Personal Audit	20											
SRA Youth Inventory	12											
Tennessee Self Concept Scale	5											
Thorndike Dimensions of Temperament	18											
Thurston Temperament Schedule	20											
The Jesness Inventory	6											
MISCELLANEOUS TESTS												
AC Test of Creative Ability	9											
California Analogies and Reasoning Test	4											
California Study Methods and Survey	4											
Chemistry Achievement Test--Anderson-Fisk												
Chemistry Test	11											
Jastack Test	8											
Lewerenz, Tests in Fundamental Abilities of Visual Art	4											
Maitland-Graves Design Judgement Test	18											
Spitzer Study Skills Test	23											

*See page 64 for list of code numbers and corresponding publishing companies and addresses.

Figure 2-1 (continued).

TEST	*PUBLISHER'S CODE NO.	GRADE LEVEL K-3	4	5	6	7	8	9	10	11	12	College
SRA Test of Practical Judgement	20											
SRA Your Educational Plans	20											
Survey of Study Habits and Attitudes	18											
Test of Study Skills	22											
Thurstone Test of Mental Alertness	20											
Vision, Hearing, and Motor Coordination	4											
READING TESTS													
Diagnostic Reading Test	20											
Durrell-Sulivan Reading Capacity	11											
Durrell Analysis of Reading Difficulty	11											
Gates-Mac Giniti Reading Tests	19											
Iowa Silent Reading Test	19											
Kelly-Green Reading Comprehension	23											
Lee-Clark Reading Readiness Test	4											
Metropolitan Readiness Test	23											

*See page 64 for list of code numbers and corresponding publishing companies and addresses.

Figure 2–1 (continued).

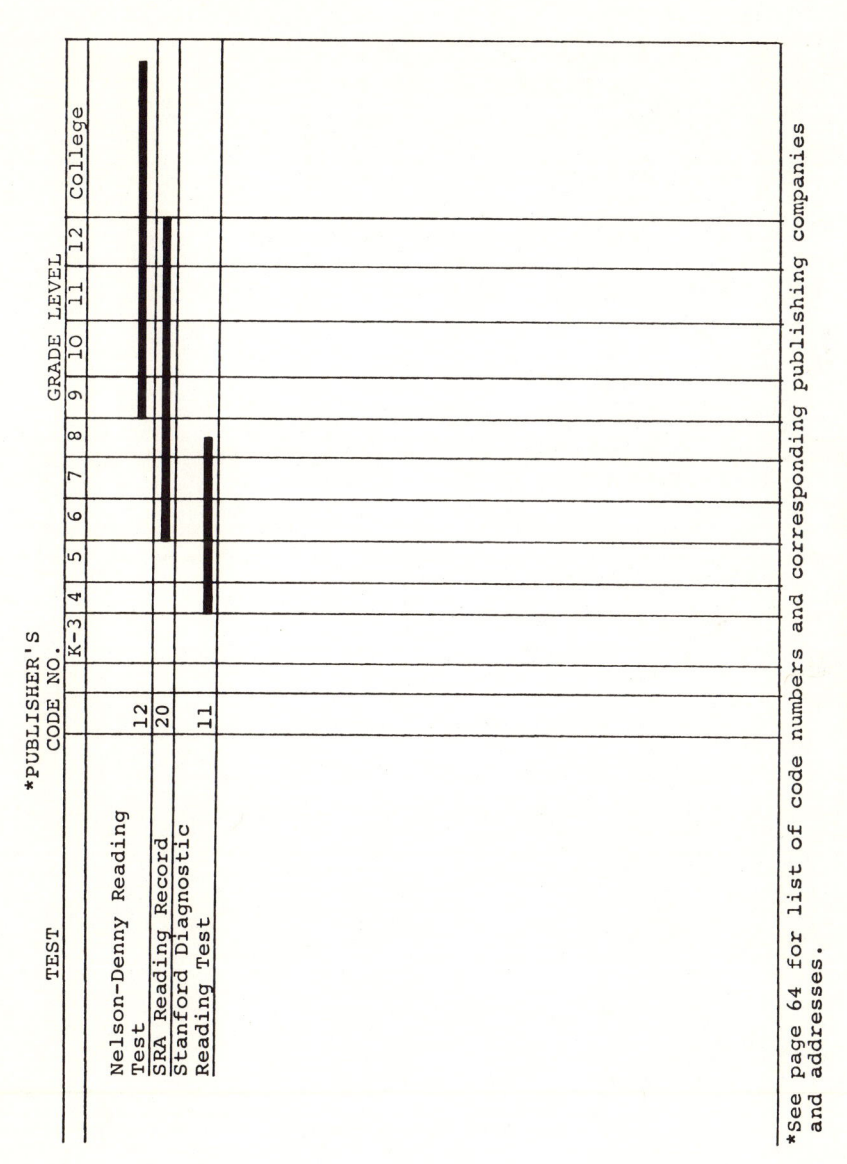

TEST	*PUBLISHER'S CODE NO.	K-3	4	5	6	7	8	9	10	11	12	College
									GRADE LEVEL			
Nelson-Denny Reading Test	12							■	■	■	■	■
SRA Reading Record	20							■	■	■	■	
Stanford Diagnostic Reading Test	11		■	■	■	■						

*See page 64 for list of code numbers and corresponding publishing companies and addresses.

Figure 2–1 (continued).

LIST OF TEST PUBLISHERS

1. The American Council on Education
   744 Jackson Place
   Washington, D.C. 20546

2. The Bobbs-Merrill Company
   4300 W. 62nd Street
   Indianapolis, Indiana 46206

3. Bureau of Educational Research and Service
   State University of Iowa
   Iowa City, Iowa 50010

4. California Test Bureau
   Del Monte Research Park
   Monterey, California 93940

5. Counselor Recordings and Tests
   Box 6184 Acklen Station
   Nashville, Tennessee 37212

6. Consulting Psychologists Press
   577 College Avenue
   Palo Alto, California 94306

7. Cooperative Test Division
   Educational Testing Service
   Box 999
   Princeton, New Jersey 08540

8. Educational Test Bureau
   Nashville, Tennessee

9. Education Industry Service
   1225 E. 60th Street
   Chicago, Illinois 60437

10. Executive Analysis Corporation
    76 Beaver Street
    New York, New York 10005

11. Harcourt, Brace and World
    680 Forrest Road, NE
    Atlanta, Georgia 30325
12. Houghton Mifflin Company
    666 Miami Circle, NE
    Atlanta, Georgia 30324
13. Joseph Jastak and Sidney Bijou
    1526 Gilpin Avenue
    Wilmington, Delaware 19806
14. Institute for Personality and Ability Testing
    1602 Coronado Drive
    Champaign, Illinois 61822
15. McKnight and McKnight
    U.S. Route 66 at Towanda Ave.
    Bloomington, Illinois 61701
16. Personnel Press, Inc.
    188 Nassau Street
    Princeton, New Jersey 08540
17. Psychological Test Specialists
    Box 1441
    Missoula, Montana 59801
18. The Psychological Corporation
    304 E. 45th Street
    New York, New York 10017
19. Teachers College Press
    Teachers College, Columbia University
    New York, New York 10027
20. Science Research Associates
    259 E. Erie Street
    Chicago, Illinois 60611
21. Stanford University Press
    Stanford, California
22. The Steck Company
    Austin, Texas

23. World Book Company
    Yonkers-on-Hudson
    New York, New York
24. Slosson Intelligence Test
    Slosson Educational Publications
    140 Pine Street
    East Aurora, New York 14052

3

EDUCATIONAL AND VOCATIONAL INFORMATION: KEEPING STUDENTS INFORMED

Another guidance service upon which considerable emphasis has been placed is the information service. The primary function of this service appears to be one of assisting the individual student to discover information which he can relate to his personal needs. This function is usually accomplished by exposing the individual to stimulating and interesting information which is related to educational, vocational, or personal-social areas of interest. It seems logical to say that if this is the primary function of the service, then there are at least three aspects of this function which are of considerable importance.

First, it appears that a focus of attention must be placed upon securing information in educational, vocational, and personal-social areas. Second, it seems that once this information is secured it must be classified in a systematic and meaningful way so that it is easily accessible and can be easily filed and re-filed. Third, it is reasonable to assume that if this information is to be used it must be disseminated in a variety of ways which will be both meaningful and practical to those who use it.

CLASSIFYING INFORMATION

Since most of the primary sources of securing information are readily covered by textbooks in this area, it seems appropriate to go directly to the second major problem, namely, that of classifying information. Here, the person held responsible for the classification of information will be faced with the problem of selecting a system which will meet a variety of criteria. One such criterion might logically be recognized as that of economy—the economy of time as the counselor is confronted with filing new information or re-filing recently used information. Other criteria which might be recognized as essential to a good classification system are the selection of a system which will be easily understood by students, one which presents a variety of information in a simple and meaningful way, and one which is flexible enough to function with equal efficiency as information increases and the classification system expands to meet this growth.

Once the person in charge of the information service has arrived at a point where he is ready to consider the classification of materials, he usually has thought seriously about (1) developing his own system, (2) purchasing a classification system which has already been designed by someone else and is available through a publishing company, or (3) placing the entire responsibility for classification in the hands of the school librarian.

If a person develops his own classification system, it may be based on such things as (1) subject matter areas, (2) areas of vocational interest as indicated by some interest inventory, (3) a library classification system, or (4) the alphabet.

Although these systems do not parallel one another, they do afford the person in charge of classifying information the opportunity to set up some meaningful system of classification. Of course, it must be realized that information classified according to subject matter areas or areas of vocational interest reflects only a small percent of the total occupations available and is therefore considered objectionable by some who use classification systems. The library classification system, although seemingly unlimited in scope, is difficult to use effectively since information is disseminated over a broad area in the library. The alphabetical system, although unlimited in scope, is difficult to use because major areas and sub-areas of classification are unique to the individual who develops such a classification system. This simply means that the counselor or the person responsible for classification will have to carry out personally the responsibilities for filing new materials and re-filing used materials. Classifying information this way is, in itself, a most time-consuming responsibility and one which cannot be done by anyone who is not completely familiar with the unique self-developed system for fear of rendering the entire system inoperable.

Sometimes a classification system is selected because it is widely used by private publishers and government agencies. A system which would fall into this category is the DOT, Dictionary of Occupational Titles, classification system. This multi-volume source contains the most complete listing of job titles presently existing. Volume I contains a definition of titles plus a comprehensive description of the occupational classification code and the occupational group arrangement; Volume II lists not only an occupational group arrangement of titles and codes but an alphabetical arrangement of areas of work and an alphabetical arrangement of worker trait groups. One reported weakness of this classification system is that students have difficulty finding information and re-filing it after they use it. Nevertheless, it must be noted that although the system does pose some problems, its assets seem to outweigh its liabilities.

AN INTERESTING INNOVATION

A system which was recently devised by Science Research Associates is one of the most unique and interesting approaches yet presented for the filing and dissemination of occupational information. The system utilizes an Occupational Scanner which consists of a number of plastic transparencies cataloged according to four areas: (a) Education, (b) Word Ability, (c) Number Ability, and (d) Interest.

A master transparency serves as a guide for scanning within the confines of each of these four areas. Scanning is done by superimposing subsections of each area over the master transparency. For example, under the area of education you have four choices: (a) 12th grade or less, (b) grades 13–14, (c) grade 16, or (d) grade 16 plus; under the areas of Word Ability and Numerical Ability you have transparencies which reflect ability in terms of (a) low, (b) average, or (c) high. When these three areas, Education, Word Ability, and Numerical Ability, are combined with Interest areas they can then be superimposed over the master transparency to reveal code numbers. These master code numbers correspond with numbers placed on a series of 400 occupational briefs published by SRA and assist the individual not only to isolate areas of interest which fall within the confines of his interests and abilities but also to point out areas which, when improved, will provide even greater latitude for him in his attempt to reach decisions relative to his future.

THE DISSEMINATION OF INFORMATION

The third major problem, that of disseminating information, appears to be relative to the amount of interest reflected by faculty members and their desire to utilize old methods and promote new methods of carrying this information to students. Although much effort has been expended during the past years to work out suitable and adequate methods of disseminating information, relatively little has been done to improve upon ways of disseminating information.

IDEAS THAT SEEM TO HAVE MERIT

Recent research by Gutsch and Logan [1] has pointed out a speculatively interesting way of using newspapers as a means of disseminating occupational information. In their research, they recognize a need for greater cooperation among school counselors, employment counselors, and newspaper writers. Through a team approach, the authors of this study feel that guidance

---

[1] K. U. Gutsch and R. H. Logan III, "Newspapers As a Means of Disseminating Occupational Information," *Vocational Guidance Quarterly* (March, 1967), pp. 186–90.

workers can assume a major role and assist in establishing the guidelines for occupational articles while employment counselors focus on areas in which occupational information seems to be most necessary and newspaper people write articles at a level commensurate with the reading ability of the audience seeking this information. Such articles could be placed in newspapers each week, thus exposing the reading public to fifty-two different occupations each year.

Another approach to disseminating occupational information is through the utilization of a group approach in which college students or high school students can meet and discuss their interests within a group setting. Group leaders might logically encourage career people who pursue the same or compatible areas of interest to serve as group consultants.

A third approach which has been of real interest and which is rather unique is the sound filmstrip. At the present, Guidance Associates of Pleasantville, New York (10570), publishes a series of vocational sound filmstrips which are of great interest to high school students. These filmstrips appear to be among the most interesting and entertaining of all audio-visual materials and can be quickly and easily utilized with individuals or groups. Although few counselors realize that these materials exist, they now appear to be an effective and necessary part of assisting to narrow the field of occupational choice. A list of current sound filmstrips is always available simply by contacting Guidance Associates.

A fourth approach which seems of interest to students is when two representatives from the same interest area discuss, within a small group setting, some of the more intimate feelings and experiences they have found within their occupational areas. Such an approach gives students who are already somewhat oriented occupationally, the opportunity to explore some of the more intricate aspects of their chosen occupational field. It also permits a certain flexibility which serves the interests of students well because it gives them the opportunity to interact with the group representatives as well as among themselves.

A fifth approach which is used quite frequently within our

setting is that of visitation and exploration. Through the cooperative efforts of employers throughout the community it has been possible, after narrowing the field and exposing a student to occupational briefs and filmstrips, to introduce a student to professional, semi-professional and skilled people who spend the entire day showing this youngster what they do and how it is done. Such a direct experience has done much to assist students with their decision making.

Perhaps much of what has been said could be modified slightly to avoid appearing inflexible. It might be wise for the counselor to remember that these five ways of disseminating information are not fast and rigid principles that must be followed precisely but rather that they are methods which others have used and have found successful. They remain flexible in that they can be modified or altered whenever such a modification or alteration will provide new methods of disseminating information. The person who has assumed the responsibility for the information service might well keep in mind the fact that when students screen information, especially occupational information, some of this information will be eliminated because the occupations are not socially appropriate; other occupations will be eliminated because they are not possible and still others will be eliminated because they appear undesirable. Although there are many theories relative to occupational choice and methods of disseminating information, research has given us considerable understanding of our limitations in these areas and further discussion regarding such theories would probably be more confusing than enlightening.

HOW TEACHERS MIGHT ASSIST

Sharing vocational, educational, and personal-social information with students seems to create a fraternal bond between teachers and their respective students—a bond which helps students to realize that the objectives and interests of the school reach beyond the four walls of a classroom. If this is true, at least to the extent to which it now appears to be true, then the problem faced by guidance counselors involves an exploration of methods of operation which will assist the total faculty to become more involved and more committed as members of the guidance team. One of the guidance responsibilities which might normally be assumed by a classroom teacher involves methods of disseminating information. Since the classroom teacher has close contact with large groups of students who are interested in relating subject matter to reality and since she is in a position which not only alerts her to student needs but permits her to serve as a model image for students, she becomes a vital link between the counselor and the student.

Naturally, in utilizing a classroom-centered approach for the dissemination of information, there is always some danger that teachers may place greater emphasis upon those types of vocational or educational information which lend themselves best to their own immediate interests. However, it must be realized that such an attitude is usually an exception to the rule and that essentially, teachers contribute whatever they can to the welfare of students because they have a profound concern for students.

Gaining Teacher Cooperation

Perhaps the greatest single challenge faced by the counselor as he embarks upon this venture involving the dissemination of information is to get the cooperation of the faculty. Essentially, his problem is one which involves many and varied human encounter situations. If such relationships as occur in these situations are to be meaningful, it now appears that they will have to be reciprocal in nature and to have as their focal point a plan of action which encourages counselors to introduce materials and ideas which will contribute to the teachers' instructional programs while asking them, in turn, to assist with the dissemination of guidance materials.

One way of approaching this problem is to assist faculty members in working out specific methods for the implementation of an information service. For example, teachers at the elementary school level might be encouraged to introduce information through the utilization of specific filmstrips or films which relate not only to the world of work but to the significance of education in that world. Once students have such a general orientation to the world of living, teachers can encourage further exploration by identifying the vocational and educational experiences of people with whom they come into daily contact. This might include an exploration of what a person must do to become a teacher, a postman, a truck driver, and/or a cafeteria worker. From time to time and through the efforts of the counselor, it will be possible to bring into the school setting individuals who will discuss their own career patterns. Opportune moments for such explorations are frequently presented through planned teacher-pupil trips to fire stations, police stations, libraries, industrial settings and business establishments.

For the upper elementary grades and on into the junior high school, occupational exploration may be facilitated through class projects which utilize the efforts of both counselors and teachers as they design exploratory experiences in an effort to investigate the many and varied roles of such major community operations as transportation, utilities, and service occupations. Once students become actively involved in gathering and sharing such information, they seem to develop a more personalized impression of what school is all about and what their commitments must be if they are to meet with success in the world of work.

As junior and senior high school students begin to formulate definite ideas about what they want to do, counselors can assist them in their initial efforts through the utilization of objective tests and comprehensive summary reports such as those explored in Chapter 2, "Mastering Effective Evaluation Techniques: How to Communicate Results."

Developing an Occupational Monograph

One of the more creative types of experiences which is easily integrated into the classroom situation is the preparation of an occupational monograph. The essence of such a monograph is based on those areas of interest, capability, aptitude, and past achievement reflected by each respective student and incorporated into his personal summary report by the counselor.

In order to add structure to an assignment of this nature, students may be referred to such guides as Hoppock's *Outline for the Study of an Occupation* [2] or *Guidelines for Preparing and Evaluating Occupational Materials.*[3]

Through the process of collecting and synthesizing information relative to such a monograph, students are brought face-to-face with the everday requirements of the occupations they are studying. Such a consciousness of these occupations causes them to reassess their own capabilities and deficiencies and creates for them a realistic situation in which they begin to commit themselves to certain specific responsibilities in an effort to get from life those things which they feel are most important to them. Ultimately, through such an exploration, they begin to ask such questions as, What kind of person am I? Where can I go after I finish high school? What happens to dropouts?

At the completion of an assignment such as this, counselors and faculty members should be willing to acept the idea that for some students such an exploration will continue to assist them to narrow their respective fields of choice while for others, it will bring some apprehensiveness and doubt. Those who are vague about where the money is to come from for further educational purposes or what vocational schools will take a person who has only a moderate record of accomplishment will find the counselor of assistance in personal conferences.

In attempting to get the support of classroom teachers for such a project, the counselor may want to point out the following values which seem to be of intrinsic importance to most learning situations:

1. They involve students in experiences which call for personal involvement and are likely to become more significant in terms of an active kind of learning—a type of learning which is meaningful in terms of total life expectations and anticipations. When this type of learning situation is developed, students are

---

[2] Robert Hoppock, *Occupational Information* (New York: McGraw-Hill Book Company, 1963), pp. 427–45.

[3] *Guidelines for Preparing and Evaluating Occupational Materials* (Washington, D.C.: National Vocational Guidance Association, 1964).

more likely to relate other aspects of the curriculum to their own patterning of relationships and ideas.

2. They place students in reality-testing situations where they use facts and information they have personally gained to check out choices or potential choices.

3. Students learn to utilize a variety of resources in order to gather the information they seek.

4. Students develop skill and competency in writing and expression. It is one thing to gather information; it is another thing to organize, synthesize, and communicate such information in a meaningful way.

5. Through supervising the preparation of the assignments such as the occupational monograph, the alert teacher can become aware of individual students who may need special assistance

6. Any one of the assignments may provide a basis for other exploratory activities.

7. Once completed, the results of some activities, such as the monograph assignment, may represent excellent occupational information. As such, this information may be placed in the guidance information file for further use by all students.

LOOKING AT THE GROUP APPROACH

It seems that of the many approaches used in guidance for the dissemination of information one of the most sophisticated is the attitudinal group-centered approach. Within the confines of a small group setting it is possible to convey many ideas that might otherwise go without recognition. It is a setting which permits students to explore experientially the responsibility of remaining in school and the consequence of dropping out of school—it is a setting which permits students to explore the immediate problem of moving from the academic world into the world of work. However, even more important than this is the fact that it is a setting which permits a student to explore the world of expectation and those demands it makes upon its youngsters. From a group setting a student can develop an element of understanding which serves as a personal sensitivity to life itself. He might learn through such an experience that in a democratic form of government such as we have in America today, a job can provide a man with self-respect—a feeling of self-worth and dignity. He may well learn that those who are without a job and without an education eventually reach a point in their thinking which tells them that they have *no contribution* which their economy values —no contribution which they can exercise to gain societal respect. Further, it is through such small group settings that students are encouraged to explore the consequences of prolonged unemployment on society and it is through such groups that they begin to understand the significance of involvement and commitment. The challenge for the counselor is to understand group dynamics and how to use such a guidance approach to the best advantage of his respective setting.

4

USING A GROUP APPROACH EFFECTIVELY

Perhaps one of the greatest challenges confronting a guidance counselor today is his ability to define and utilize groups in a meaningful and sophisticated way—a way which will serve not only as an advantage to students who are group participants but to faculty members, administrators, and community members who ultimately experience the effectiveness of such group relationships. However, before a counselor can actually become effective in the application of group techniques, he must have a basic understanding of the theoretical implications for his work. Unlike other concepts in guidance, the theories of human encounter are more susceptible to modification—more susceptible to change as it is introduced through the constant research of those many counselors who have committed themselves to the development of better guidance programs. In an effort to establish a basic frame of reference from which to work, counselors should realize that authors have sometimes defined group guidance as a personal service made available to three or more individuals having common or similar problems. Although such a definition might be considered adequate when making a general statement about group guidance, it would appear that such a definition might not permit one to develop a vivid and irreversible concept of group guidance when it is compared with such terms as group work, group psychotherapy, group counseling, and multiple counseling. In view of these implied semantic complexities, it might be advantageous at this point to investigate each of the terms involved and their unique features.

SOME DISTINGUISHING MARKS OF GROUPS

Of the many terms to be considered, the term "group work" is perhaps the most inclusive of all types of group activities since it is indicative of a broad variety of methods of providing group experiences. This is especially true if the term is defined as any type of work consisting of an assemblage of three or more persons who are engaged in meeting a common objective while at the same time maintaining and enhancing the unity, fraternity, and understanding necessary for, and essential to, a productive way of life. Of the many group activities that can be classified under the term "group work" then, each seems to have a uniqueness relative to the ultimate purpose for which the group is designed.

Group guidance, as one type of group work, is probably the term most frequently used in our public school setting. Despite its apparent popularity, it remains a term surrounded by ambiguity. The difficulty in clarifying the term "group guidance" seems to stem from the fact that some authors have recognized it as more closely related to, although not synonymous with, a therapeutic approach.

Pursuant to the latter concept are those definitions introduced by Bennett and Hoppock in their writings. Bennett has, for many years, maintained that purposes, techniques, and the relationship to counseling, rather than content, are basic criteria in classifying a group activity as guidance.[1] Hoppock simply implies that group guidance provides a common background of related information that improves counseling.[2] In essence, it might be said that group guidance has many characteristics. However, from a profound exploration of literature devoted to this subject it now appears

---

[1] Margaret E. Bennett, *Guidance in Groups* (New York: McGraw-Hill Book Company, 1955), p. 5.

[2] Robert Hoppock, *Group Guidance: Principles, Techniques, and Evaluation* (New York: McGraw-Hill Book Company, 1949), pp. 5–7.

that the following characteristics give group guidance a quality unlike that of any other type of group work:

1. The person who assumes the responsibility for the leadership role usually does so as a consultant or resource person who provides a flexible leadership role which becomes increasingly stronger whenever it appears that such leadership is necessary.
2. The group is composed of normal individuals who appear to have a common purpose.
3. The attitude of each member of the group toward other members of the group usually undergoes some modification which is then reflected through a permissive and accepting atmosphere within the group.
4. The format for each group setting is usually relative to the purpose of the group, thus permitting more structuring with groups that pursue an interest in educational and vocational areas and less structuring with groups that pursue an interest in specific problematic areas.
5. The group is usually flexible in size depending upon the purpose of the group, thus permitting certain groups such as those placing a major focus of attention upon educational and vocational interest areas to vary in size with such a variation relative to the attitudes of the group members and their ability to adjust to, and interact within, a large group setting.
6. Interaction by group members usually varies along an intellectual-emotional continuum starting, in most instances, with a discussion of a problem of an academic or intellectual nature and progressing to one of an emotional or feeling nature.

Close observation of these characteristics will permit one to see a distinct difference between group guidance and (1) group psychotherapy, which involves a group consisting of from seven to eight people who are united in a profound emotional setting and function under the leadership of a person who assumes a role which is classified as neutral but not passive, (2) group counseling, which involves a group of approximately eight people united in a less profound emotional setting than group therapy and which permits each member of the group to reflect his own unique problem while at the same time assisting other members of the group to face individual conflicts which are too difficult for any one of them to solve alone, and (3) multiple counseling, which involves a small group setting in which the leader must lose his identity as the leader and is actually viewed by members of the group as a member himself.

IMPLEMENTING GROUP GUIDANCE

The technique for implementing group guidance requires considerable skill especially if the group is to meet with success. During the past few years, many individuals have considered testing programs and orientation programs to be group guidance. Perhaps this has been a serious mistake, for although it may well be that these programs can be classified in this area when carried out properly, it seems obvious that more effort must be made to relate these activities directly to guidance. When activities of this nature are unrelated, they reflect nothing more than the broadest concepts of group work and fail to convey the idea that group guidance is never taught as are academic subjects, nor is it carried out by people who are not professionally trained in the area of guidance.

If we assume each school setting to be unique in itself, the actual details involved in working with groups will be relative to the needs of the students. Some of the areas in which group guidance services can be of value have been recognized by Hoppock as falling into the following categories:

1. Orientation—helping a person become acquainted with a new environment.
2. Educational Guidance—helping a person plan his education.
3. Vocational Guidance—helping a person plan a vocation.[3]

---

[3] Hoppock, *Group Guidance*, p. 3.

Perhaps it would be desirable to consider personal-social problems along with these first three areas since guidance has expanded sufficiently over the past few years to make this area of vital importance.

As was pointed out before, it might well be said that the actual size of the group is relative to the purpose of the group. Thus, when working with personal-social problems it is perhaps best to use small groups of seven to ten students and to increase group size when working in educational or vocational areas since these last two areas seem to permit individuals within the group to adjust to one another more easily.

For the most part, it appears that the formation of a group takes place when individuals gather or are asked to gather in an effort to meet a need or accomplish a task. Glanz states that, "three major types of psychological needs appear to be operating in the formation of any spontaneous group: (1) protection, (2) enhancement, and (3) action." [4]

In a group guidance setting, individuals are brought together through educational, vocational, and personal-social areas of interest. These interests can later serve as the basic premise upon which the objectives or goals of the group are founded. If these objectives are clearly stated and well defined, the group can move ahead by outlining the steps necessary to achieve these goals. If on the other hand, the group fails to recognize clear-cut objectives, it may be wise to discontinue the group until these objectives can be clearly stated. In essence then, it appears that the success of the group is directly related to the objectives set by the group as well as by the ability of the group to define these objectives. It is probably true that as the group moves toward a level of maturity, i.e., a better understanding of others and a greater tolerance for others, objectives are sometimes modified to become more accessible to each individual within this setting.

---

[4] Edward C. Glanz, *Groups in Guidance* (Boston: Allyn and Bacon, Inc., 1962), pp. 39–40.

THE TECHNIQUES INVOLVED

The areas which appear to be best suited to group guidance have already been listed as orientation, educational planning, vocational planning, and personal-social development.

In the area of orientation, the following techniques are sometimes considered helpful:

1. Visitation—The visitation is designed to permit the individual to visit a junior high school while attending the elementary school or possibly to visit a college campus while attending a high school. Visitations of this nature become group guidance when individuals are permitted the opportunity to discuss in groups the problems involved in the transition.
2. Student Handbook—The handbook is used to transmit information to the student. It can be used as a technique in group guidance if groups of students are permitted to clarify understandings and problems as related directly to the information found in the handbook.
3. Group Conference—Conferences of this nature are meaningful when counselors, teachers, or administrators visit the school or schools from which new students have come. They can be used as a technique in group guidance when students who have already made the transition are permitted to discuss with potential students problems which might occur during or after the transition.
4. Assembly Program—If the assembly program consists of a special program by an outside speaker or by students during which individuals in the group or audience are permitted the privilege of discussing problematic areas or points of concern, this would constitute group guidance. If on the other hand the speaker indoctrinates the group concerning what he considers important, this constitutes group work.

These are only a few ways in which orientation becomes group guidance. As individuals become increasingly familiar with the orientation program and with group guidance, variety frequently enters into the picture and serves as a keynote to success in the development of better group guidance.

The techniques employed to unite groups relative to educational, vocational, and personal-social areas are many and varied.

Educational Planning—In educational planning, for example, groups will form because of their interest in, or need for, information regarding courses, electives, major and minor areas of concentration, scholarships, fellowships, loans, and placement opportunities.

Vocational Planning—In vocational planning groups form because of individual interests in common areas of work. Information which assists the individual in focusing his interest is usually disseminated prior to the time that the student has reached the dropout age. The general interest of the group is usually related to community opportunities, and students within the group are often bound together because of similar interests as related to these opportunities. Other techniques which seem to reveal common group interests are achievement tests, aptitude tests, interest inventories, questionnaires, autobiographies, and personal interviews. These common interests which serve as a basis for the formation of a group will be closely related to the type of information received by the individual through the school's information service, the way in which this information has been disseminated (i.e., posters, clippings, newspapers, audio-visual aids, career days, assembly programs, visitations, career clubs, and community surveys), and the limitations placed on this information.

Personal-Social Development—Groups formed for personal-social development consist of individuals who have united because of problems and/or interests in self-understanding. Some of the techniques used to discover these areas of common interest are autobiographies, personality inventories, problem checklists, questionnaires, and sociometric techniques.

THE PRINCIPLES INVOLVED

From the foregoing discussion then, it appears that the principles involved in group guidance are these:

1. Group guidance is effective only after the objectives of the group have been clearly stated and well defined.
2. Group guidance serves as a supplement to, not as a substitute for, individual counseling.
3. Group guidance best serves students of similar age levels and with similar problems.
4. Group guidance is best carried out by individuals who have been professionally trained to undertake such responsibilities. This training can be in the form of academic training oriented toward professional guidance status or it can be carried out in the form of extensive in-service training oriented toward a group guidance point of view.
5. Group guidance is performed in groups which vary in size depending on the nature of the problem and the stated objectives of the group.

In essence, it appears that the focus of group guidance should be determined by the particular needs of that group and that the person responsible for the leadership function be a permissive, accepting, and understanding individual.

Specifically, it might be said that a group guidance approach can provide, for each group participant, a better understanding of what he is and how he relates to the world in which he lives. Such an understanding might logically consist of a realistic knowledge of what the world of work is like, the role of education and its significance to the world of work, an understanding of those personality characteristics which make life a pleasant experience, and the steps which become essential if a group participant is to move from where he is to where he wants to go.

In a previous chapter, emphasis was placed on narrowing the field in terms of intelligence, achievement, interests, aptitudes, personality characteristics, and disabilities. Utilizing such an approach in order to group students makes it possible to form fairly homogeneous groups, whose participants have a sense of compatibility which will permit them to explore, in concert, such things as educational plans, vocational decisions and/or personal-social adaptations. Once such groupings have been made, group participants might be called together during homeroom periods or study hall periods. It now appears that such groups can function on an attitudinal basis and that they might most appropriately meet once a week for a period of fifty minutes. If the period is any shorter than this the effectiveness of the group may be hindered. This, of course, is not to say that shorter periods cannot be effective but rather to say that it now appears that the greater the length of time the greater the sharing of the group. In essence, it might be said that time serves to assist in establishing cohesiveness especially when group members are concerned about personal problems. For educational and vocational exploration, groups may be just as effective when they meet for thirty-five minutes. Since the objectives of the group are different and since there is less emotional involvement, it seems that such decisions must be made by each respective guidance counselor who serves as a group consultant.

VOCATIONAL-EDUCATIONAL ACTIVITIES

Counselors are frequently concerned about group goals and how they might best be established. If we can assume for a moment that such goals may first be recognized as educational, vocational, and personal-social, it is then possible, through narrowing the field, to bring individuals together who have something in common. The greater the ability of the counselor to select participants who share a commonality of existence the greater the cohesiveness of the group. Once a group is formed, it may be rather awkward to change group participants unless the participants themselves acknowledge the need for such a change.

After groups have been formed counselors can pursue a number of activities which are both interesting and meaningful to group participants. As an illustration, groups designed to explore educational-vocational interests might find the following recommendations interesting and effective:

    a. Bringing in consultants from universities who will work, plan, and create an atmosphere which will assist students and parents to understand better what higher education is like and what it means in terms of personal development.

    b. Bringing in discussants who assist students in their exploration of post high school education other than college.

    c. Bringing in discussants from junior colleges and permitting them to elaborate on opportunities available through *terminal* and transfer programs.

    d. Bringing in discussants such as officers from local unions who would be capable of introducing information about apprenticeship programs within the immediate area and throughout the state and the entire region.

    e. Bringing in discussants such as USES counselors who might discuss on-the-job training opportunities available to students who drop out of high school and those opportunities available to students who complete high school.

Emphasis in each case will be in terms of where a student can go with the educational training he has, where he might go with additional educational training, and how well his abilities lend themselves to such educational training plans.

GROUPS FORMED FOR PERSONAL EXPLORATION

Whenever groups are formed for the purpose of exploring personal problems, much consideration must be given to the emotional tone of the group. One approach which has been extremely successful with students is the attitudinal group-centered approach.[5] The primary focus of such a group is directed

---

[5] Kenneth U. Gutsch, "Group Guidance: An Attitudinal Approach," *Guidance Journal,* Vol. VI, No. 1 (Summer, 1967), pp. 184–90.

toward developing a better understanding of one's self as well as developing one's poise in personal contact experiences with others.

The basic medium through which these purposes become manifest is that of a loosely structured discussion centered around topics of mutual interest to the group generally on some aspect of personal concern to one or more members of the group. Such a discussion usually does not pursue an intellectual or theoretical line but presumably relates to the personal concerns of one or more members of the group. Similarly, group members are responsible for initiating questions related to personal growth and for limiting the conversation, in general, to matters pertinent to these feelings or attitudes. It is also helpful if topics or feelings discussed are of personal concern to someone in the group rather than of interest only as an abstract or academic issue.

The limits of the group are set by the material presented. That is to say that this sort of group setting might also be applied with educational-vocational explorations but that it might be restricted to shorter periods of time per meeting. Experience now indicates that with personal problems these meetings are more productive when extended to periods of fifty minutes. Students will usually prefer to operate on a relatively unstructured basis, being guided by varying expressions of individual group members who wish to obtain group concepts on matters of personal concern. The responsibility for leadership during these sessions may reside with the counselor who is already familiar with group techniques or may be rotated to fit the needs of the group.

As to specific procedure for initiating a discussion within the group, the following ideas may be helpful:

1. Individual members may contribute a brief biographical sketch, indicating their experiences in performing teaching functions.
2. Individuals may request some reaction to personal questions involving attitudes or values.
3. Individuals may be interested in a group response to problems in interpersonal relationships followed by a series of sessions devoted to examples or feelings perti-

nent to each problem area. Occasionally a review of common manifestations of personality weakness as observed in these groups will provide a basis for self-examination by each member of the group.

The basic assumption relative to such a group approach is that group members will, as practitioners in the art of interpersonal contacts, feel a continuing sense of need to improve their skill and understanding of how relationships develop and how and why individuals react in the ways they do. It is a generally accepted psychological principle that the greater the degree of one's attitudinal self-understanding and acceptance, the greater one's acceptance of and insight into the emotional needs of others. If this basic assumption is correct, it appears that one of the best approaches for assisting students with personal problems is through an attitudinal group setting in which the student first gains personal insight and understanding and then is able to use this knowledge to assist others in gaining the same experience.

PRE-COLLEGE GUIDANCE

One technique which has been extremely effective with college-bound students is a small group approach which utilizes as a basic frame of reference the topics of pre-college orientation and financial aid for college-bound students. Much of this information has been placed in two publications by Chronicle Guidance Publications, Moravia, New York. The first publication is a compilation of information entitled College Charts, which enables the high school student who is college bound to get sufficient information so that he can ask questions and explore more profoundly those areas of academic and personal interest that each institution of higher education offers. The second publication is entitled Student Aid Annual and supplies a student with information on financial aid programs, range of aid, requirements for aid and application deadlines. It also contains information relative to the availability of on-campus and off-campus employment and earnings.

Although this service has been available for many years and

is a regular part of the Chronicle Guidance subscription service, few counselors have used this information as a means of developing greater latitude and facility in the thinking of students who are college bound.

Through group approaches such as these, students are frequently stimulated to a point where they request individual counseling services. Perhaps one thing we should *not* dismiss from our thoughts is the realization that just as there are group settings which pave the way for individual counseling services, there are some instances in which the client will profit from individual counseling services before he can benefit from group experiences. This is particularly true when an individual is moved into an attitudinal group guidance setting. Experience with such transitions now indicates that students who have received individual counseling services are more comfortable in such a setting and are more capable of talking freely about themselves and their problems. To understand how each of these functions can serve the other in a mutual bond of reciprocity, one must first understand counseling—not as an intellectual sparring match but rather as a functional challenge involving the application of didactics. As an illustration of how counseling can be utilized effectively within the school setting, the next chapter explores with the reader those ideas, innovations and realizations which seem essential to such effectiveness.

5

COUNSELING: IDEAS, INNOVATIONS, AND REALIZATIONS

Much of what is done in counseling sessions today involves both educational and vocational exploration. It is because of the emphasis placed on accurate educational planning and vocational decision making that a focus of attention must now be directed toward personal factors which might serve as distractors when a student seeks to pursue his educational-vocational interests, i.e., toward those personal characteristics which so frequently make the difference between success and failure in the world of everyday living. Regardless of where the client is on the developmental continuum, certain factors seem extremely important in determining the extent to which he reaches his desired objectives. One of these factors is, of course, his educational background and how well it lends itself to such objectives. Another factor is his personal attitude toward others. A third factor is his ability to utilize his potential for growth to his best advantage. A fourth factor involves his interest and a fifth factor involves his intelligence. All of these factors play a significant part in defining for the client what he is like and how he functions within the confines of his own unique world.

IDEAS

The Problem of Impulsivity

In a relationship which is designed to assist the counselor in arriving at an objectively defined image of the client—an image of impressions gained through testing—the relationship itself gains breadth from the objectivity. Since most students are "normal," their responses to tests and inventories focus on points which are of greatest significance to their personal lives. It must be remembered that there are times when students perform poorly on tests as a result of some temporary disorder rather than a permanent disability. Occasionally students perform poorly in academic areas and on tests not so much because they are not bright but because they are highly impulsive. This means that they react negatively to certain experiences which they feel are not compatible with their thinking. At moments like this the reaction is rather spontaneous and irrational. When a student reacts this way he is usually penalized. If he is in the process of taking a test, he may respond in an irrational way throughout the test simply because he did not like one of the first questions. If he does not like the teacher he may react by leaving the classroom prematurely or he may act out against the class in order to be removed and thus get away from concepts with which he does not agree or cannot cope. Although such irrational actions have been difficult to understand until recently, the advent of the Neuroticism Scale Questionnaire and the How Well Do You Know Yourself Inventory have done much to define these characteristics and make it possible for counselors to learn more about working with impulsive clients.

Once a counselor has established a good working relationship with the client, he can counter this tendency toward impulsivity by assisting the client to understand impulsiveness and how it works against him. Usually such an explanation is introduced within the Summary Report and the explanation itself serves, to some degree, as a counter to the condition. A student who has been impulsive should be encouraged to maintain his relationship with the counselor until the counselor is reasonably sure that the client understands and can counter his own impulsivity.

The Problem of Depression

When students are extremely ambitious but feel that they will not meet with much success they reflect characteristics of depression. Although many of these students could probably function at a much higher academic level if they did not have this disability, the disability itself is not easily dealt with even after a student has been made aware of it.

Perhaps the key word here is "aware," for it reflects the idea that for a depressive, knowledge of an action is only superficial and will remain so because he does not have the courage to test this knowledge against reality and convert it into reality. Persons who experience depressive characteristics want to accomplish more than they have accomplished in the past but are unwilling to face the possibilities of rejection or defeat in making that accomplishment a reality. They are people who experience great pain because they are unable to transcend their present status; they are people who are unwilling to make an attempt to compete for a better position in life because the pain of defeat or failure is greater than the pain they experience now. In a sense this experience with life serves much as an epigain does since it nurtures the present climate of the client. In reality, however, the client sees some other climates as enjoyable but fears the pain of the journey from where he is to where he wants to go.

To work successfully with a person who experiences depressive characteristics the counselor must consider those objectives which the client is most willing to attempt. By setting objectives which he can accomplish with ease the counselor manages to desensitize the client and counter his disability by introducing successful experiences. Later, the counselor can introduce more difficult objectives.

The Problem of Precounseling Orientation

Although counselors are familiar with various types of orientation programs, they have probably not done much thinking about precounseling orientation. Perhaps they have many times thought about how wonderful it would be to have a student understand how counseling services might help him before he actually requested the services. Such an approach to counseling has been utilized with the Presbyterian Guidance Program for a number of years.[1] If, as a counselor, you are located near one of the many

---

[1] *Presbyterian Guidance Program Handbook* (Richmond, Virginia: Board of Christian Education, Presbyterian Church of the United States, 1963).

Presbyterian Guidance Centers situated throughout the United States, you can visit with these people and learn how your services within the school setting can complement the services offered by these centers. The people who coordinate these centers have not used this approach to replace those services offered by school counselors but rather have attempted to supplement such services. These services, as they are offered by the Presbyterians, are primarily concerned with an indoctrination period which utilizes adults who serve as aides to students. These aides do much to assist Presbyterian students to understand how counseling and testing are used to orient them to lifework situations. It seems, as one contemplates such an indoctrination period, that the experiences offered by these services can assist school counselors equally well. Actually the contact that students have, first with aides and then with counselors from Presbyterian Guidance Centers, is quite brief. Since it is limited in time, many of these Presbyterian counselors would probably be pleased if they knew that public school counselors were continuing the work they initiated at their centers.

If such a service is not available in your community it may be possible to develop an aides program by appealing to parent groups. Through such efforts, it may be possible to establish a group of aides who can offer a service which complements that offered by the Presbyterian Program.

This, of course, is simply one approach to precounseling orientation. Adults who are interested in carrying out an indoctrination program or a precounseling orientation program such as this may also be recruited from other religions or from the ranks of the faculty. The important thing is to form a group of adults who are willing to assist youngsters as they begin thinking about their transition from the purely academic setting to the lifework setting.

Establishing a Precounseling Orientation Service

The first step in the establishment of such a program is to make sure that it is approved by the administrators and parents. As a second step, the counselor must consider proper coordination of such a program. If he is capable of coordinating the program without placing himself in a line position, i.e., an administrative position, relative to his relationship with other faculty members, then there would be no reason why he might not assume this position.

As a third step the coordinator of precounseling services and the counselor, if these two people are not one in the same, might attempt to establish a group of aides. These people might be drawn from any of the sources discussed earlier. That is, they may be drawn from religious groups, from the school settings, from professional and business settings or from any other sources of mature and responsible human beings. Normally, one adult aide can work successfully with approximately five students. However, it should be remembered that the number of aides can be modified at any time. If the ratio is more comfortable when smaller, this adjustment can be made at the discretion of the coordinator.

The fourth step might include an in-service training program for aides and would most appropriately afford the counselor an opportunity to introduce consultants who could be brought in for discussion periods and to introduce materials, i.e., those occupational briefs, educational catalogues and other things that seem important to a precounseling service.

As a fifth step, it seems highly important to consider what method of operation aides will use in the presentation of materials and how they can best facilitate this responsibility.

INNOVATIONS

Human Encounter: A Discerning Journey

Perhaps of the many things the counselor does, the most challenging is the one which confronts him as he enters into a counselor-client relationship. Realizing that the relationship is of primary significance, he never really knows how the client feels. In reality, he experiences many speculative moments, each unique and each revealing, for it is only through such contact that the counselor becomes conscious of what this person—this client—is really like. As an antecedent to understanding a client, the counselor must understand what precedes the counseling relationship and how this affects the relationship itself.

During the past few years there has been much speculation about what precedes the counselor-client relationship and what transpires within the confines of such a relationship. If for a moment we can agree that individual counseling involves two people, one of whom is professionally trained in counseling and another person—a "normal" person—who by virtue of need seeks the specific services the counselor renders in order to experience personal and positive growth, then it is possible to accept a general frame of reference from which we can begin our exploration.

What Precedes the Counseling Relationship?

Naturally, each relationship is unique, yet many theorists now believe that when an individual seeks assistance from a counselor it is because his present behavior repertoire is inadequate.

What a student actually experiences as an antecedent to his initial contact with a counselor appears to become manifest through a sequence of events the first of which transpires when he becomes involved with a problem which he can neither resolve nor ignore. As a result of this situation he develops tension. The tension distorts his perceptual field and this, in turn, causes him to relate rather awkwardly to the world around him. His new relationship—that is, his changing relationship with this world—creates for him a more demanding situation in which he feels he must either explain his change to the satisfaction of society or control his reactions relative to change. Essentially, what he seems to experience is a period of self-examination—a period during which he feels he must evaluate himself and determine how he relates to the world around him. If, as a result of this examination, he cannot understand himself and cannot control the changes he feels are taking place, then he is in trouble.

In effect, it appears that behavior is a product of experience, perception, and generalization. To an existentialist the experience of the moment is perhaps of greatest psychological significance. Yet it is not difficult for me to understand that this is just one fleeting moment of a man's total existence and that his total existence is based on events of the past which intrude themselves into his present. It is not difficult to realize that what this student experiences at this moment of existence is only the current phase of a process that began a long time before. To understand the emergence of this experiential syndrome is, to me, the essence of understanding MAN for it includes the whole story of MAN's existence and acknowledges patterns of life experiences which, in themselves, are reflective of his moment of existence. Yet, even as a student experiences this moment, he lives in anticipation of what is yet to come—the vagueness of his tomorrow reaches deep within him and touches his never-ending curiosity. As he enters the office of the counselor he experiences not only the pain of his personal difficulty but the anticipation of his new relationship, and it is in this setting that he must explore the possibilities of the journey from where he is to where he wants to go. In reality, a journey created as much from the fantasies of his personal anticipation as from the "facts" of his experience. A journey which is totally real to him during each moment of his experience simply because he sees not only with his eyes but with his mind—and what he sees in his distorted state of existence creates a distance between himself and those around him. Each day, his world becomes smaller and he becomes more and more isolated—each day he becomes more involved with himself and less involved with those around him. When he finally seeks professional assistance, his cry is one of desperation—it begins deep within him and permeates the totality of his entire existence—it is a message of need the profoundness of which is compounded by years of personal experiences. Perhaps it is only at such a moment as this, a moment during which the client sits before us, that we can appreciate the impact of our relationship on his journey back to the reality, the stability and the security found through self-understanding.

Ideas Within the Counseling Relationship

When considering the fact that the experiences a student has once he becomes a client are projected and become manifest within the relationship, it is not difficult to visualize these projections as attitudes which are reflected for or against attitude objects. In their simplest form they are nothing more than momentary feelings about ideas, events, or situations while in their most profound form they become undercurrents for basic themes which seem to become the major forms of attention throughout the counselor-client relationship. As an example of what sometimes happens within the relationship, take the following statement which was introduced by a young woman during an initial interview:

> I feel like I'm destroying myself... I don't feel like I'm necessarily being destroyed... but like I'll eventually destroy myself.

As this statement was originally introduced, it was considered a simple thought reflected by the client. The profoundness of this client's feelings is perhaps best reflected by the consistency with which this idea is repeated. When it was followed by similar statements during the second interview, it began to look as if it was one of the dominant strains within the interaction setting. During her third interview she said:

> I've about decided... that this is, uh... I mean, I think it's over for me... I've gone a little too far to ever turn back.

The theme now seems obvious; the client is, in her deepest moments of thought, contemplating suicide. If, as a counselor, you can appreciate the idea that at this moment she is unwilling to assume responsibilities and that her unwillingness does, in itself, communicate a message, then it is possible to counter her attitude toward self-destruction. This assumes a more determined position than some counselors are willing to accept. However, if a counselor is truly a professional person, and there is no reason that he should be considered anything other than this, then it appears that the decisions he makes to counter the attitudes of the client will ultimately be in the best interests of the client. It is not merely a matter of wanting to or not wanting to share the responsibilities of the client, it is a matter of understanding the impact that pre-established societal conditions have on this person and then assisting her to recognize how they influence her life.

As a basic example of how you might utilize such an approach let me introduce a statement which seems common to counseling situations: "I hate my dad." Although this statement appears truthful at the moment of experiencing, it must be recognized that the client who makes a statement such as this is a composite of experiences and that this feeling of hate may only be a reflection of an immediate relationship or experience with his dad. It may also be true that this feeling of hate has been reinforced recently and with a certain amount of consistency—yet, it also seems that the client is not utilizing his total experiential pattern for understanding this relationship and is only relying on his immediate feelings to make such an evaluative statement. Since the counselor must attempt to assist the client to arrive at a realistic sense of understanding he might at the moment the client says "I hate my dad" respond with, "You now experience a relationship with your dad which you feel could be improved; yet, there were times when this relationship was better than it now is—times when you felt it offered you what you needed in a father-son relationship."

A natural response by counselors and theorists at this point might be, "But what if the relationship was always poor?" Although this is possible, it appears that an individual seldom requests assistance from a counselor unless his ability to cope with a situation has reached total exhaustion. Also, it seems that there are degrees of "goodness" and "poorness" and that the client's judgment of the present situation is based on a premise of better experiences in the past. Further, it doesn't seem possible that two people could live together for any length of time without sharing some good moments. Therefore, when the counselor responds in this way he accomplishes several things. First, his statement gives the client the opportunity to recall a better relationship with his father. Second, by asking the client to explore a more positive phase of his relationship with his father the counselor has introduced a counter catalyst—a conceptualization which, although not threatening, has caused the client to reexamine the more positive aspects of his relationship with his father and in doing so has caused his own feelings of anger toward his father to dissipate. Third, since the client's feelings now vacillate between what is and what was, the client is motivated to re-examine his feelings in an effort to arrive at an understanding of what is realistic. Fourth, since the client now recognizes that his feelings toward his father are not consistent, he must explore what transpired within the relationship which caused him to feel as he does about the relationship. Fifth, as a result of such an exploration the client does, of necessity, recognize that he is, in fact, one of two parties involved in the relationship and therefore is not only influenced by the relationship but also influences the relationship.

REALIZATIONS

Theory and Practice in Action

Perhaps one of the few ways to learn about neurotic anxiety [2] —to explore and understand the anxiety syndrome—is to study anxiety as it is actually experienced. Naturally, this is not always possible. However, if one can capture the essence of such an experience in writing, then it may be possible to assist those who are interested in understanding interaction settings to experience vicariously the impact of an anxiety oriented situation. The case of Tony is such an attempt. This is a unique case in that the initial contact lasted for approximately three hours and ultimately served as the only contact the client made with the counselor until after he graduated.

The Case of Tony

Late one afternoon, a young man entered the counseling office requesting personal services. He introduced himself as Tony, shook hands with the counselor, sat down, and began to talk.

---

[2] R. May, *Psychology and the Human Dilemma* (Princeton, N.J.: D. Van Nostrand Company, Inc., 1967), p. 105.

From observation it seemed that he was perspiring profusely—a point of extreme interest since the building was completely air-conditioned.

After listening to him discuss his feelings, it appeared to the counselor that Tony might be experiencing acute anxiety syndrome. His anxiousness seemed to be reflected in statements relative to his lack of sleep, his need to pace the floor, his feelings of apprehension, and his feelings of low self-worth. These statements seemed supported by such observable conditions as his constant perspiring within the confines of a well air-conditioned atmosphere, his apparently defensive laughter at the nature of his problem, his physical expression of internal discomfort which he sometimes described as "butterflies" in his stomach, and his very presence in the counseling office for the purpose of personal counseling services.

In listening to Tony tell his story, it appeared that the thematic pattern he reflected might best be explained in terms of acute anxiety and anxiety affect. As Tony states:

> My doctor encouraged me to seek additional help . . . he said my problem doesn't seem to be physical . . . yet, I feel that I can't sleep . . . I don't know what to do . . . the doctor has given me tranquilizers . . . my blood pressure seems to be up . . . I guess it must be my academic work that's bothering me. I'm a student here at the University. I'm completing my work on my degree, but I'm not sure that I can do it.

This first statement by Tony seems to become more meaningful when considering his overall external appearance. From what he has introduced in his initial statement, i.e., those internal conceptualizations he has presented, and what he reflects in his appearance, i.e., those external physical conditions he experiences, it appears that his present academic situation may be creating for him some moments of discomfort. Actually, what he is reflecting in his conversation and through his physical appearance appears to be anxiety affect—the second of *four* parts of an anxiety experience, i.e., anxiety cue, anxiety affect, primary anxiety reaction, and adaptive reaction.[3] In this case it appears that Tony's thoughts or memories and feelings of anxiousness most probably precipitated the surge of emotion which Tony was feeling at the moment he made his initial statement. Since he has, at this point, experienced the first two parts of the anxiety experience, i.e., anxiety cue and anxiety affect, it seems logical that the counselor should begin to explore the relationship more profoundly in an effort to determine where the client is with respect to primary anxiety reaction. That is to say that as the counselor continues to work with Tony, it seems logical for him to attempt to find out where his client is in terms of the total anxiety experience. As a result, the counselor now begins to look for a defense or withdrawing move by the client.

As the discussion continues:

> *Counselor:* You feel that the academic situation in which you now find yourself is causing you to experience some feelings of discomfort.
>
> *Tony:* I . . . I don't know. I've been married and I'm now divorced. My wife and I were never really happy together, except for the first few months. I met her in California. After six months of marriage there was little left. We traveled to different parts of the United States, first to Illinois and then to New Hampshire . . . I wanted to continue my schooling and to become a lawyer. She wanted to go home . . . her home is in Wisconsin. After I felt we couldn't get along, we left New Hampshire and went to Wisconsin where we lived next door to her parents. Her parents were on one side and her relatives on the other . . . God, what a mess! The thing is that I was only 22 years old and I was making $11,000 a year and she kept telling me I wasn't a success (pause).
>
> *Note:* The client seems to vacillate here and introduce another major pattern of interest. Perhaps he

---

[3] Frederick F. Lighthall, "Anxiety as Related to Thinking and Forgetting," *What Research Says to the Teacher,* No. 30 (Washington, D.C.: American Educational Research Association of the NEA, 1964), p. 5.

attempts to avoid the pain of exploring his original theme.

Counselor: Her attitude toward you was discomforting at times.

Note: The counselor encouraged the client to continue his pattern of thought, feeling that eventually the client would probably bring these two themes together.

Tony: Damn right it was... she kept telling me that I wasn't ever going to make it and that I couldn't ever buy her the things she wanted... her parents are wealthy, you know (pause).

This experience which the client has just related seems to complement a concept recently introduced by Ellis in his conceptualization of Rational Therapy. Ellis introduces the idea that a client does not of necessity feel guilty for what he experiences but rather because he thinks it criminal for him to have these experiences.[4] This seems more of a conflict between pre-established standards such as one might normally find in a society, and the latitude with which these standards are enforced by the affected person.

In this case, Tony appears to feel that he has failed his wife—a failure which relates not so much to the condition failure as it exists within the confines of his own mind, but rather to the condition failure as it is established within the confines of the new fraternal constellation of relatives in which he now finds himself. In essence, his embarrassment relative to his relationship with his wife seems to result from the fact that he feels he is unable to reflect a personal image for his relatives which is indicative of his adulthood—his ability to accept and handle responsibility related to the proper financial support of his family. Strangely enough, he also realizes a strong sense of accomplishment in his present occupational endeavor which pays him

---

[4] A. Ellis, "The Essence of Rational Therapy," in *Counseling and Psychotherapy,* ed. Ben N. Ard, Jr. (Palo Alto, California: Science and Behavior Books, Inc., 1966), p. 95.

$11,000 a year. Yet, in the opinion of his relatives, it is his very lack of financial stability for which he must feel a sense of guilt.

> *Tony continues:* She claims her father was the only one who knew her... (mumbles) I'm glad someone did.
>
> *Counselor:* Your relationship was not so good as you would have liked it to be.
>
> *Tony:* No, for six months before I left we had no sexual relationship. She couldn't ever be satisfied sexually or any other way... I've had other women though ... I always felt that I was capable of satisfying women... no one ever complained before.
>
> *Counselor:* Your wife was satisfied with the relationship for the first few months which seems to indicate that she was not unhappy sexually... and then things changed... she seemed less responsive and wanted to return home. You took her to Wisconsin hoping that this effort would improve your relationship with her, but actually the relationship became worse. Now, you not only experienced a dissonance within your relationship with her but a dissonance in the relationship with her parents and other relatives.
>
> *Tony:* Yes, they made me feel that I was wrong.
>
> *Counselor:* Wrong?
>
> *Tony:* You know! They made me feel that wanting to continue my education was wrong... that my job was not paying enough... that... I don't know.
>
> *Counselor:* It's difficult to say...
>
> *Tony:* ... that I wasn't good enough.
>
> *Counselor:* And you've had this feeling before.
>
>> *Note:* The counselor now attempts to recapitulate—to reintroduce the cue, the thematic pattern related to the client's initial statement regarding the academic idiom. Originally, the client's anxiety affect indicated that something challenging existed with which the client had to deal. The counselor realized that the client had either to master the situation in which he found himself or in some way escape from a condition which placed him in a situation which was painful and/or humiliating.

Tony continues: Yes . . . strange I should recall this now, but I felt this same feeling . . . but not so strong . . . I was in grammar school and the teachers, that is, most of the teachers, seemed not to like me . . . except one . . . this one was very close to me.

Counselor: Perhaps much like your situation now . . . perhaps you have one professor who is rather supportive.

Tony: Exactly . . . exactly like my position now. That's amazing! I hadn't thought about this for years.

Counselor: Your situation now seems to parallel your earlier experience.

Tony: Yes, definitely . . . (pause).

Counselor: Your teacher then had great faith in you just as your professor now . . . (pause—no reaction) . . . perhaps you now wonder about this faith she had.

Tony: Yes, (pause) . . . I failed her.

Counselor: And now you're in a comparable situation and don't want to fail your professor.

Tony: Yes . . . now I'm in the same position and don't want to fail my professor.

Counselor: . . . nor yourself.

Tony: I made up my mind that I would continue . . . and I will. I won't run away. I'll stay. I've already made up my mind.

Note: He is herein referring to the duplicity of his existence [5] . . . the desire to run away and the desire to stay. In effect, it becomes a struggle to stay and as such reflects more vividly the attempt to speculate relative to the consequences of withdrawing from his immediate situation. Such withdrawal would constitute the third part of his anxiety experience, anxiety reaction. Although this reaction could also be reflected in a defensive or diversionary way, his immediate concern seems to be one of withdrawal.

Counselor: It now appears that you are struggling with the idea of running away. Is it because you now know

---

[5] H. Kaiser, *Effective Psychotherapy,* ed. Louis B. Fierman (New York: The Free Press, 1965), p. xxii.

that the characteristics you reflect—the symptoms of sickness you have—are another means of escape? If you were sick, you could leave the University and there would be no loss of self-respect . . . no personal embarrassment . . . you could leave the University without having failed the professor . . . If you were sick, the professor would accept the fact that you dropped out of school . . . he would still have faith in your ability to perform . . . (pause) . . . a faith which you, yourself, seem to lack.

Note: This is an attempt to counter the client's thinking. If the client is using sickness as a means of moving away from his present situation, this statement will alert him to the fact that the counselor realizes what he is attempting and as a result he will not continue to use this method.

Tony: No . . . I made up my mind to stay and I'll stay.

Note: The client at this point appeared rather adamant and perhaps was deeply hurt by the counselor's statement. Yet, it seems obvious that if he had actually reached a decision to stay, he would not continue to imply the alternative of running away.

Counselor: It's difficult for you to admit that your physical symptoms may be a convenient way of moving away from a situation which seems to be quite pressing.

Tony: (Long pause) It's like a crutch, isn't it? I've been using it . . . yes, it's hard for me to face this . . . mostly because the professors here have expressed faith in me and I don't want to disappoint them. They make me feel good . . . I've earned good grades . . . God, I'd hate to embarrass them.

Note: Tony now appears to be moving toward the fourth part of the anxiety experience, adaptive reaction. Here for the first time during this three-hour marathon interview he seems to understand his actions and feelings more profoundly than ever before.

Counselor: And yet, the responsibility is not entirely yours . . . you were personally encouraged to remain as a student . . . you were encouraged to continue because you received good grades and this was objective proof of their encouragement... so if there is disappointment, it must be a reflection of dishonesty... you seem to imply that these people were not honest in their assessment of your capabilities... and yet, could they be anything other than honest?

Tony: I never thought of it that way but that's true... God, that's a relief... it's a relief to know that I was acting in a natural way... it's like sharing my burden.

The third part of Tony's anxiety experience was reflected by his attempt to withdraw through the utilization of sickness as a diversionary means of escaping without any serious repercussions.[6]

The fourth part of his anxiety experience seemed to become activated by his insight—his realization that the medical doctor may have been correct in assuming that he was really not physically ill, but rather using illness as a personal convenience. This part of the anxiety experience is unlike the first three parts for it occurs much less frequently and requires the courage for personal self-exploration. Tony's courage, at least in part, was probably maintained through the interpersonal approach subscribed to by the counselor. Understanding anxiety and knowing what had to be done seemed of the essence. Realizing that Tony's feelings of tension, torment, despair, horror, panic and uneasiness, were actually part of an anxiety experience, it was possible to assist Tony to explore these feelings which ultimately ended in adaptive reaction, i.e., a state of adaptation. Perhaps his most painful experience involved attending to the belief that he actually wanted to continue as a student while at the same time wanting to flee from the pain of the experience. Recognizing the fact that his emotional urge was not without cause, Tony had the courage to search his past for a better understanding of why he felt as he did. As a result of this search, he was capable of exploring childhood memories which seemed to complement his

---

[6] H. P. Laughlin, *The Neuroses* (Washington, D.C.: Butterworths, 1967), p. 58.

present academic situation. Having found such an experience, it was possible for Tony to explore the relationship between this past situation and his present feelings of anxiety. Since the reward for such an exploration seemed to exceed the pain caused by no exploration, Tony was motivated to continue his search. The adaptation which he experienced through this search permitted him to continue on in school until he received his degree.

At the present time he is working and appears to find much satisfaction in the challenges introduced by his job.

Counseling and the Guidance Program

In conclusion, we might say that counseling is the very heart of the guidance program. It utilizes the other services and provides the student the opportunity to develop a realistic concept of his "self" and his role in the world of everyday living. It is based on the proposition that—

> 1. Every human being has worth. This is an axiom which underlies social and political democracy and most of the religious and humanistic traditions. It follows from this axiom that people who work with others (students, for example) in a helping relationship try to discover the worthiness in those they are serving. This is sometimes difficult, especially when the student is using unattractive ways of asserting himself or of gaining attention or is suspicious of the person trying to help him. The implications for counseling are many. One is that the counselor must strive to recognize his own biases and try to control them.
>
> 2. Behavior is caused. Every act of behavior, including sudden impulsive acts and seemingly irrational acts, has an underlying reason or reasons. Frequently, it is impossible to discover the reasons. One implication for counseling is that we gain nothing by merely condemning a breach of discipline or an attitude which is out of line with the socially accepted pattern. This is not to say that the counselor condones unacceptable behavior, but rather that he can be much more effective in helping the student find

the best path if he tries to understand the student and help him understand himself.

Another implication for counseling is that one must search for the patterns of behavior by putting together the pieces in the jig-saw puzzle of behavior. The counselor does not make judgments based on a single act but rather takes note of each act as a clue to the larger pattern.

3. People can learn and grow and develop only to the extent that they feel secure and accepted. Since counseling is a process which encourages individuals to learn to understand themselves (just as classroom teaching is primarily a process in which people are encouraged to learn about various aspects of the world they live in), it follows that the counselor needs to do all he can to create an atmosphere in which the counselee can feel secure and accepted. If the counselor or teacher who is talking with the individual student feels that he is not going to be lectured to, or punished, or threatened; that he is going to be listened to within reasonable limits of available time; that the counselor sees him as a worthwhile person, even if some of the things he has done and some of the attitudes he has taken are not accepted—then a solid basis for the counseling relationship has been established.

4. Each of us behaves and feels and reacts to situations according to the way he perceives himself and the world around him. By perceives is not meant just our visual images, but our understanding of all that is happening to us. Often these perceptions are different from the objective reality. From this it follows that a counselor can be much more helpful to a student if the counselor can find ways of getting as close as possible to the student's way of seeing his world and himself.[7]

Role of the Counselor

As reflected by Carl Rogers, the role of the counselor is to assist the client in using his own resources to solve his problem. The concept here is that "... the individual has a sufficient ca-

---

[7] State Department of Education, *Better Guidance Better Schools: A Handbook* (Florida: State Department of Education, 1959), pp. 43–44.

pacity to deal constructively with all those aspects of his life which can potentially come into conscious awareness." [8]

Some counselors believe that the most effective means of facilitating the counseling process is as follows:

1. The counselor should create an atmosphere of acceptance so that the pupil feels free to express himself.
2. The counselor should be empathic, not sympathetic; e.g., a counselor should understand a pupil's feelings of self-pity, but should not share them.
3. The counselor should be nonjudgmental. He should not show approval or disapproval of a pupil's attitudes or behavior.
4. Although a counselor's attitudes should be consistent, his expectancy should be flexible in order that he may meet the variations and complexities of problems.
5. Since the goal is to increase self-understanding and self-direction of the student, the counselor must allow the pupil to make his own decisions.
6. The counselor should help the pupil to understand the normality of having problems without underemphasizing the importance of the problem.[9]

Along with this, some points to be considered when counseling are that:

1. Within the interview itself, the first goal is to put the pupil at ease, to help him relieve or reduce his tension.
2. This cannot be accomplished unless the counselor himself is relaxed and does not try to hurry or push the pupil. Untrained counselors may be tempted to interrupt the pupil's verbalization or even to take over the conversation.

---

[8] Carl Rogers, *Client-Centered Therapy* (New York: Houghton Mifflin Company, 1951), p. 31.

[9] Kentucky Department of Education, *Educational Bulletin*, Vol. XXVI, No. 9 (September, 1958), p. 892.

3. The interview should not be a cross-examination or a lecture. Some pupils find it difficult to express themselves. Such cases will require more participation at first from the counselor.
4. Questions which require only yes or no answers are not conducive to free expression on the part of the pupil.
5. The pupil should have the individual attention of the counselor. However, the attention should not be intense.
6. A good counselor keeps the conversation on the pupil's level in content and vocabulary.
7. Many problems cannot be solved in one interview. Sometimes much harm results from a counselor's trying to accomplish too much in one interview.
8. A good counselor is aware that the pupil's statement of his problem may not be the real problem. Or the stated problem may be only one facet of a complexity of problems.
9. It is usually a good idea for the interview to end with a summary of what has been accomplished and what remains to be done.
10. Generally speaking, the solution to a problem follows a pattern such as:

   a) statement of the problem.
   b) organization and objective consideration of the problem.
   c) consideration of possible sources of action and possible results.
   d) choice of the best course of action with alternative plans.
   e) evaluation of course of action with possible modification of plans.[10]

---

[10] Kentucky Department of Education, *Educational Bulletin,* Vol. **XXVI**, No. 9, pp. 892–93.

LEVELS OF HUMAN ENCOUNTER

Levels	What is done?	Who does it?	Required Educational Background
Interview	Building a face-to-face relationship in which getting or giving information and getting acquainted is of primary concern.	Most frequently in schools it is done by teachers.	No specific education or academic background necessary other than some experience with interviewing techniques.
Advisement	Giving information which has been subject to some interpretation and is applicable to normal teacher-pupil or teacher-parent relations. Increased skill necessary.	A teacher with some understanding of his personal limitations and/or a teacher-counselor with some knowledge of the skills necessary and the referral resources available.	No specific background is required; however, it is hoped that the person advising will have some training in the behavioral sciences with an understanding of his own experiential and academic limitations.
Counseling	Primarily this work involves assisting "normal" individuals through their own efforts to gain a better self-concept.	A professionally trained guidance counselor who has gained state certification or an individual who is a mem-	Graduate training in the behavioral sciences with some emphasis on guidance and counseling. This includes a

114

Counseling (continued)	It consists of establishing a person-to-person relationship in which one person who is professionally trained assists a second person who needs help in educational, vocational, or personal-social areas of adjustment.	ber of Division 17 of APA and has also met the minimum certification standards set for guidance-counselors in his state.	background of supervised training in the form of a laboratory experience and/or an internship experience plus the specific knowledge and training necessary to implement broad testing services which will eventuate in a testing program.
Psychotherapy	Attention is usually focused on severe behavioral problems through the use of projective and other techniques reserved for clinicians who have been properly trained to use such techniques.	Clinical psychologists or counseling psychologists who are recognized members of the American Psychological Association or an association with equal status.	Graduate training with a primary focus of attention in the area of psychology and with great emphasis on a profound knowledge of projective and clinical techniques used to assist individuals with serious adjustment problems.

Counseling Defined

If it were possible to arrive at a logical definition of counseling from the ideas which have preceded, it might be said that counseling seems to involve five basic elements: [11]

First, individual counseling involves two people, the counselor and the client, who are engaged in interaction.

Second, the client is considered a "normal" individual who may have problems involving vocational decisions, educational plans, and/or personal-social adaptation.

Third, the interaction experienced within the counseling setting usually permits the client sufficient latitude to discuss freely those ideas or events which appear to be significant to him at the moment of interaction.

Fourth, the relationship is governed by certain specific conditions, i.e., it is established at the request of the client and is characterized by privacy, confidentiality, set time limits and regularity.

Fifth, the primary purpose of the relationship is to bring about the best possible utilization of what he already has. The client is encouraged to explore the world in which he lives and the way in which he relates to this world.

Ultimately, counseling is probably related to other types of human encounter situations which seem to be differentiated from each other as they become functional. Perhaps one way of summing up such a differentiation is through the utilization of the preceding chart which compares levels of human encounter.

---

[11] K. U. Gutsch, "Counseling and the Experiential Syndrome," *Counselor Education and Supervision* (Summer, 1967), pp. 317–18.

6

WORKING WITH YOUNG STUDENTS

Although the nature of guidance as it is found at the elementary school level is not totally unlike that found at the secondary level, there are conditions and situations at the elementary school level which appear to be more compelling than they are at any other level. Perhaps the primary reason for this is the fact that many of the problems which high school students experience actually had their origin at or prior to the time they entered school.

Counselors must begin to realize that the word Guidance acts like a magic word which does, in fact, convey hope to thousands of parents who have children in need of help. Yet, there are many ideas which remain to be explored before these children actually receive the assistance they need.

SEX DIFFERENCES

As an example of what we must yet learn, few counselors recognize the fact that there are definite sex differences in the adjustment, behavior, and mental health of boys and girls. Boys, it seems, not only experience greater difficulties within the confines of social adaptation but also seem to have personal problems which are more pronounced than those of girls.

Then too, few counselors seem to realize that when students are evaluated by teachers there is a sex bias which favors girls over boys. As Kaplan put it:

Recent studies affirm this observation. There appears to be a halo effect at work in the awarding of grades to children. Quiet, docile, obedient behavior is rewarded with high marks, while the aggressive, resistant behavior commonly displayed by boys is more likely to antagonize ... Furthermore, since boys do not adapt so well to quiet, orderly classroom routine, they experience considerable thwarting in school. This results in emotional reactions which influence test performance and results in lower achievement scores.[1]

DISORDERS LEADING TO POOR READING

Another concern for counselors might most appropriately include that of detecting dyslexia.[2] Since educators frequently estimate that visual disorientation affects about 15 to 20 percent of students, it seems imperative that counselors explore more profoundly those characteristics which identify the syndrome normally reflected by poor readers. Although some indication relative to the detection of poor visual perception was introduced in Chapter 2 in the subsection "Looking at Intelligence Objectively," it now appears that there are other disorders which are more difficult to detect because the student experiences such severe distortions that he is never really recognized as a reader at all. One such disorder is dyslexia which, in its simplest form, might be defined as brain damage caused by brain injury or degeneration. To recognize this disorder, the counselor must become familiar with those characteristics most frequently reflected by a dyslexic. These include:

a) Displacement in writing such as CMAL for the word CALM.
b) Displacements in reading such as STOP for SPOT.
c) Reversals in writing such as Ǝ for E.
d) Confusion of letters such at IT instead of IS.

In many instances, experts have referred to this problem as word blindness—a unique type of inability which seems to pre-

---

[1] Louis Kaplan, *Mental Health and Human Relations in Education* (New York: Harper and Brothers, 1959), pp. 291–95.
[2] "Dyslexia," *Idea Reporter* (Fall, 1967), p. 6.

vent the person from reading words as wholes. This problem is sometimes compounded by the fact that the student not only fails to comprehend the word as a whole but is confused relative to the forms and sequence of the letters.

The real problem seems to be in accurate diagnosis prior to the time the individual enters school. However, since few youngsters learn to read or even attempt to read prior to this time, it seems highly improbable that there will be much emphasis on the proper diagnosis of visual disorders prior to entering school. Ultimately, the inability to properly diagnose reading problems appears to magnify problems which become manifest in poor academic performance.

Perhaps even more dramatic than the effect it has on performance is the effect dyslexia has on the emotional stability of the person who experiences it. Within the confines of the research now available relative to this subject, we find that many of those youngsters who experience such a problem also experience feelings of depression.

Since reading plays such a significant role in the lives of children who live in our society—a society where the ability to communicate is held in such high esteem—it seems imperative that counselors recognize the word-blindness syndrome and make proper referrals whenever and wherever necessary.

Detecting Dyslexia

In our personal experiences we have learned to watch for word-blindness in youngsters and have increased our potential to detect it not only through those characteristics previously discussed but through the utilization of the Wide Range Achievement Test. In their 1965 revision of WRAT, Jastak and Jastak have introduced an interesting method for detecting dyslexia. Their claim is that, "A discrepancy of more than 10 points in standard score in favor of IQ may be indicative of a reading disability. The larger the discrepancy the greater the probability of dyslexia, if the reading score is the lower of the two." [3]

---

[3] J. F. Jastak and S. R. Jastak, *Wide Range Achievement Test Manual* (Wilmington, Delaware: Guidance Associates, 1965), p. 29.

As one example of what might be found, examine the following case:

> Case: Boy, 9½ years, in the third grade
> WISC IQ—98
> WRAT Reading Grade 2.1, Quotient 77
> Spelling Grade 2.4, Quotient 80
>
> The reading quotient in this case is 21 points below the WISC IQ. The spelling grade was 2.4 with a spelling quotient of 80. The reading grade for an IQ of 98 is 4.4 which means a reduction of nearly 2½ grades in achievement. The reading grade corresponding to an IQ of 100 may be obtained from the normative tables in the Appendix. [Reference is to the 1965 WRAT Manual.] Enter the table appropriate to the age of the individual and find the grade rating for a standard score of 100. This will give the average grade achievement expected of a child of his age. If the child's IQ is above average, say 115, find the expected grade corresponding to a score of 115 which is 5.6 for a 9½ year old. The difference between ability as expressed by IQ and achievement in reading in favor of the former may be used quite effectively to establish the degree of underachievement.
>
> Group tests of a verbal nature cannot be used as criteria of reading disability since they measure the same thing. Since the perceptual transcoding takes priority over comprehension, reading comprehension tests are of little value in the diagnosis of dyslexia.[4]

Perhaps greater insight can be realized by following the case of Frank. This is a case with which we worked that may present a more logical explanation of what course of action counselors might pursue when confronted with a problem such as dyslexia.

The Case of Frank

Boy, 13½, repeating 7th grade
Slosson IQ—113
WISC IQ—118

---

[4] Jastak and Jastak, *Wide Range Achievement Test Manual*.

WRAT Reading Grade 4.4, Quotient 76
Spelling Grade 4.0, Quotient 74

The reading quotient in this case is 37 to 42 points below his IQ score. The reading grade for his Slosson IQ of 113 would be about 10.7; for the 118 WISC score his reading grade would be 11.4.

This information, combined with earlier findings which indicated that the youngster was reflecting characteristics typical of a dyslexic, made it essential to refer the client to a specialist for assistance in reading. When he was unable to adjust to the training offered within the confines of this reading experience, he returned to the guidance counselor and asked for additional assistance. Unable to do anything for the student in terms of appropriate referral, the counselor corresponded with people who were researching dyslexia. From the limited information available, he gained enough information to inspire his purchase of a Kit of three dimensional plastic letters which he felt could be used in training the client to learn to read through the tactile sense (that of touch). Through the utilization of these letters he first developed within the client a simple awareness of basic words. As he continued to work with the client, he introduced more difficult words and worked specifically with those words which seemed to lend themselves best to first and second grade readers which he brought to the laboratory for the boy to read.

Here is what transpired as related in the actual report by the counselor, Jack Stewart.

> *Session VIII*—I proceeded as planned with the program Dr. Gutsch and I had decided upon. We used a child guidance toy—a metal board with plastic letters that had magnets attached to hold them to the board. We spelled out several words letting him (the client) move the letters from one place to another to get the feel of these words and letters. We tried several words that he had missed on the WRAT as a starter. He became bored and tired after about an hour.
>
> *Note:* Because we had only one C in the set, we used a letter U turned sideways (⊂) to spell the word COR-

RECT. This was the student's idea. It should be noted, however, that after having spelled both RESULT and CORRECT previously, and having spelled them both correctly, he now spelled RESULT—RES ⊂ LT (using the U in the side position). Whether or not this is significant, I cannot tell at this time.

Session IX—The client was late for his appointment. He was talkative today. He had been tossing pennies and nickels at school and had a pocket full of change. We worked with the magnetic-board alphabet again, spelling some of the words we had worked with during the past session. We also worked with a few new words. He remembered all of the previous words except one ... for some reason he forgot how to spell the word CORRECT.

Session X—The client was on time today. This was his third time to use the magnetic-board alphabet. He is evidently proud of his progress. We were able to spell eight words correctly by the end of the session.

He combed his hair differently today ... he looked toward the two-way vision mirror and combed it several times while we were working.

When I introduced a new word he attempted to assemble the letters. He looked for my approval if he was doubtful of the next letter. I gave my approval either verbally or through a gesture ... if he was wrong, I corrected him. He assembled the words on the table and moved the words, letter by letter, to the metal board. It is in this way that we now feel that he is getting the *feel* of the words.

He seemed to realize that he was making progress.

Session XI—The client brought his own list of spelling words today. He was to have a spelling test the next day and evidently wanted to go over the words in the usual manner. They were more difficult than those words we had worked with before and there was a greater number of words. These words were to be used at the seventh grade level.

Note: The client did not do well and seemed disappointed. He took the list of words home and agreed to continue his efforts.

Session XII—I had the client read aloud out of a second grade book today. He did much better than I expected he would. Whenever he missed a word he would stop and spell it with the plastic letters and the magnetic alphabet board. He is confused about *on* and *of* and *great* and *giant*.

Session XIII—The client read a second-grade level book again today. We followed the same pattern as in the previous sessions. When the client missed a word, we would stop and he would spell the word with his three dimensional plastic letters. Today he was confused about *fur* and *for*.

Although the client has not reached any outstanding proficiency with words at this point, he recognizes two things. First, he now realizes that he has a visual problem and that he cannot fully utilize his intellectual potential until he overcomes this difficulty. Second, he realizes that we are here to assist him, not to judge him. We feel that the relationship we have is genuine and realistic and that as a result, the client will continue to progress. Perhaps, in time, he will read at his grade level. So long as we can maintain his interest, there is always hope that this end will be attained.

Since these reports the client has continued to progress. Now, twenty-three weeks after we originally started to work with him, he reads at the sixth-grade level. We hope that with continued effort he will read at the seventh-grade level before he returns to school this fall.

UNDERSTANDING SEPARATION ANXIETY

Although sex differences and visual problems are always of major concern when working with youngsters, there is still another syndrome of characteristics over which we must maintain a strict vigilance. This is separation anxiety.

Many years ago, Otto Rank introduced the idea that the prototype of all anxiety was part of the birth experience. He felt that the physiologic manifestations normally accompanying birth closely paralleled those circulatory, respiratory and other changes found in anxiety oriented individuals. Although this theory has not gained prominence, it was through these basic efforts to explain anxiety that Rank introduced the idea of separation as a basis for anxiety.

Perhaps one of the most traumatic experiences any youngster has is his first permanent type separation as he enters school. Because this separation is so important and can cause so profound an influence on the child's life, we thought that counselors should become cognizant of the separation syndrome.

Usually, the child who experiences separation anxiety is not capable of independence, i.e., of moving away from his mother. As a result of being forced to separate the child may become noncommunicative. At times he may appear retarded since he is extremely apathetic while at other times he may scream uncontrollably because he is extremely frustrated. Naturally, these are only some of the characteristics which such a youngster reflects. Yet, they are important because they are so very much like those characteristics reflected by youngsters who experience autism, symbiosis, or retardation.

Since some counselors might be capable of providing the proper climate for the growth and development of cases involving separation anxiety, but incapable of offering anything other than referral services to those who are suffering from autism, symbiosis, or retardation, it is imperative that they become capable of differentiation. This is true, not only so that proper referral is available to the student but also to assure that counselors are not attempting to practice in areas for which they have no training. This is not to say that cases involving separation anxiety should be handled exclusively by counselors but rather that this syndrome lends itself better to the type of services they offer. Naturally, if a psychiatrist is available for such cases, referral is always appropriate.

THE IMPACT OF ILLNESS ON PERFORMANCE

Many counselors seem remiss in their exploration of background information, i.e., that prenatal, postnatal and chronological information which provides a developmental pattern of understanding from which they might most appropriately work. Since many children become patients, it seems extremely important to explore the impact of such an experience on the child. Some years ago, Jessner, Blom, and Waldfogel [5] conducted research the results of which seemed to indicate that youngsters who underwent tonsillectomies and adenoidectomies experienced emotional postoperative reactions such as tics, fears, regressive behavior and bed wetting. Disturbances were also noted in habits related to speaking, sleeping, and/or eating.

If a counselor is aware of what cued a specific incident in a child's life, he can focus upon the incident and elicit the cooperation of parents and faculty members in attempting to correct the situations. Such cooperative efforts are, in many instances, much more effective than is the counselor-client relationship alone.

IDEAS ABOUT SHYNESS

Of the many characteristics reflected by children, one of the most difficult to understand is that of shyness, i.e., the tendency to move away from situations which call for personal integration. Sometimes a child who reflects shyness is neurotic—sometimes psychotic—sometimes creative. Some years ago Torrance [6] gave an illustration of a creative boy of thirteen, saying that teachers, counselors, and principals described the boy as *bright, bored, lazy,* and *withdrawn.*

In 1941, Bradley and Bowen [7] introduced characteristics reflective of schizophrenia and included in this list such things as seclusiveness, diminished number of personal interests, and regressive nature of personal interests. Accordingly, these charac-

---

[5] Lucie Jessner, Gaston Blom, and Samuel Waldfogel, "Emotional Implications of Tonsillectomy and Adenoidectomy on Children," *Psychoanalytic Study of the Child,* Vol. 7 (New York: International Universities Press, Inc., 1952), pp. 126–69.

[6] E. Paul Torrance, *Guiding Creative Talent* (Englewood Cliffs, New Jersey: Prentice-Hall, Inc., 1962), p. 83.

[7] C. Bradley and M. Bowen, "Behavior Characteristics of Schizophrenic Children," *Psychiatric Quarterly,* XV (1941), 296–315.

teristics might also lend themselves well to the extremely quiet, shy, withdrawn youngster who is creative.

The point which we are making is simply this: characteristics of shyness apparently stem from many different situations and reflect considerable divergence depending on the age at onset, the origin, and the defense used as the child devlops a self-concept. Counselors, it seems, must become cognizant of those characteristics of shyness which best lend themselves to referral. If as a counselor you attempt to enter into a relationship with a youngster who may be creative it is wise to remember that group settings are usually not extremely appealing to these youngsters. Further, there is evidence that the fashionable practice of brainstorming, i.e., having persons in a group suggest ideas in as rapid a succession as possible, is not particularly productive of unique ideas. In fact, in IPAR it is reported that the group process inhibits creative thinking.[8]

DELINQUENCY: CAN WE PREDICT IT?

Although we have not observed a sufficient number of cases to make a definite and irreversible statement at this time, it does seem that one of the best instruments for screening out potentially delinquent children is the *Jr.–Sr. High School Personality Questionnaire—Factor Q^4*, which when computed as being high, reflects a tense, frustrated, and driven student. For those who are interested, this questionnaire is available from IPAT (The Institute for Personality and Ability Testing), located at 1602 Coronado Drive, Champaign, Illinois 61820. A second factor on this questionnaire which seems to be supportive of the delinquency syndrome is *Factor D*. A high sten score on this factor indicates that the client is probably excitable, impatient, demanding, and overactive. When the two factors are high, delinquency proneness seems inevitable.

Another instrument which was designed primarily to determine delinquency is the KD Proneness Scale. The scale was developed

---

[8] "Creativity," *Carnegie Corporation of New York Quarterly*, Vol. 9, No. 3 (July, 1961), p. 5.

by Kvaraceus [9] and contains 75 multiple choice questions which are designed to differentiate between personality characteristics of delinquents and nondelinquents. A check of items covering the same area is filled out by an adult who is familiar with the child.

Still another approach which was introduced by Craig and Glick [10] utilizes the *Glueck Social Prediction Table* as an instrument which might detect delinquency. Results of this study, which covered a period of approximately ten years, seem to indicate that family factors may be as significant in predicting juvenile delinquency as are personality characteristics.

HELPING TEACHERS TO UNDERSTAND

Perhaps one of the most important phases of a counselor's work at the elementary school level is the in-service training of teachers. Within the confines of the school setting, it is the teacher who first comes into contact with the youngster and it is the teacher who must be trained to recognize the character syndrome which lends itself well to referral.

As a guideline to the in-service training of teachers, the guidance counselor may want to consider some of the following ideas:

Within the bounds of personal limitations teachers can assist the guidance program by making an effort to—

1. know and understand pupils by establishing and maintaining a working relationship with each student;
2. identify and work with individual problems through special class projects and/or various other activities;
3. assist students in gaining a better understanding of themselves and the world in which they live through the use of individual and group techniques; and
4. refer students to the proper resources whenever necessary.

---

[9] W. C. Kvaraceus, *KD Proneness Scale and Check List* (New York: Harcourt, Brace and World, 1950).
[10] M. Craig and S. J. Glick, "Ten Years Experience with the Glueck Social Prediction Table," *Crime and Delinquency*, Vol. IX (1963), pp. 249–61.

Basic to such a responsibility is an understanding on the part of the teacher as to what constitutes a working relationship and how to create such a relationship with students. Naturally, such a relationship involves a cooperative setting between student and teacher. The purpose of this setting is the creation of an atmosphere which permits growth and development through understanding and acceptance. A possible way of entering into such a relationship would be—

1. to accept the individual for what he is, not for the act he has committed.
2. to attempt to understand the individual—to know the pain and the hurt that he has experienced and thus to be *emphatic* and not *sympathetic* in the relationship.
3. to remember that the success of this relationship is in the hands of the teacher—a person who is mature enough to understand and control such a relationship.
4. to communicate through verbal and physical means a feeling of sincerity and interest at a level easily understood by the child.

When the teacher assumes a role which parallels these concepts, a feeling of security is experienced within the individual which becomes of primary importance in the establishment of a good relationship. A reaffirmation of this belief is implied in the following statement by Willey:

> The feeling of security is based on stability of expectancy. In the process of interaction between the child and his parents, the child and his siblings, the child and other children, and the child and the teacher, there is established a feeling of predictability of the type of response different patterns of behavior will produce. The feeling of security or insecurity begins early in life, normally in expected and predictable patterns of interaction between mother and child. The mother expects certain behavior on the part of the child and the child expects certain behavior on the part of the mother. In other words, there appears to be an adjustment and personality reorganization in meeting the requirements of other people.

> The key to developing a sense of security is "consistency." A child is happier under a severe and autocratic teacher, if she is consistent in every instance, than if he is under an erratic, unpredictable, inconsistent teacher who is "strict" one day and "laissez faire" the next. Children who do not know what to expect may develop into anxious, neurotic, and fearsome individuals.
>
> Feelings of security in the child are strengthened by a feeling that he is liked by his immediate family, by his teacher, and by his classmates. Hence, normal adjustment requires one or several other human beings. A child who is loved, has friends, and belongs has an unassailable feeling of his own value; in the absence of such love, however, a child's life is marked by strong feelings of insecurity. Demonstrations of loyalty, sympathy, understanding, and consideration appear in very young children and continue throughout life.[11]

Teachers can assist children to experience this human touch if they will trust themselves and trust the children. Through such trust they will find their own techniques coming readily to hand. It appears that this friendly atmosphere is one upon which most teachers thrive. And yet, this is not enough; teachers must do even more.

> In every group there are some children who need more than an overall protective dose of friendliness. Every child needs a lot but in most cases there is at heart one who needs an especial amount.
>
> The child is usually easy to pick out. He may seem the least lovable child. He may be the dirty child or the noisy one or the slow one or the quiet child who is so easy to forget. This child you may want least is often the child who needs you the most....[12]
>
> Thus we may conclude that the need to achieve, the need for a feeling of independence, and the need for social approach can all be summarized under the heading of a

---

[11] Roy D. Willey, *Guidance in Elementary Education* (New York: Harper and Brothers Publishers, 1952), pp. 119–120.
[12] *Ibid.*, p. 121.

need for a feeling of adequacy. Closely integrated with these needs are the needs of affection and belongingness which contribute to the feeling of security.[13]

This then, is the role of the elementary teacher who by virtue of her training works in the field of human relations and serves as one of the most effective links in the chain of allegiance dedicated to assisting students. Truly, this is a most important role and one which is served at a time most vital in the student's life. The significance of this role at the elementary level becomes even more vivid when emphasized by Knapp's statement:

> To delay the use of guidance practice and techniques until entrance of the child into secondary school is to overlook the fact that the child has been growing and developing for approximately twelve or thirteen years previously. Giving guidance and directions to the growth of children in these years preceding entrance into the secondary school may prove to be more important than that provided at a later date. Many of the maladjustments that develop during the secondary school years may be prevented altogether if good teaching and good guidance have functioned effectively for the child while he was in the elementary school. The early years of the child's life are certainly the formative years. Good guidance during these years may develop patterns of extreme importance in shaping the child's entire life.[14]

Kaplan further clarifies the teacher's role by saying:

> Teachers play a great many different roles in the lives of children. These may be classified roughly into professional roles and personal roles. As a professional person, the teacher must have a scientific, objective knowledge of children, be skillful in teaching methods, and competent in the technical aspects of the educational process so that he can act as a judge, referee, counselor, inspector, source of knowledge, group leader, and representative of society.

---

[13] *Ibid.*, p. 125.
[14] Robert H. Knapp, *Guidance in the Elementary School* (Boston: Allyn and Bacon, Inc., 1959), p. vi.

Equally important is the personal role of the teacher in the classroom. By the very nature of his position the teacher is a parent figure, an object of identification, a target for conferences, aggression, and displaced hostility, and a source of emotional support. Teaching is one of the few occupations where the practitioner's professional success is so closely related to his personal qualities. Teachers retain their effectiveness as professional persons only so long as they remain warmly human, sensitive to the personal needs of children, and skillful in establishing effective relationships with them.

There is evidence that a well-adjusted, mature teacher who is professionally competent and can establish rapport with children may have a positive influence on their mental health.[15]

Perhaps most teachers are already aware of the proposition that in order to do a better job of teaching it is necessary to gain a better understanding of the individual student. In an effort to attain such an objective, school administrators have, for many years, promoted the use of cumulative record forms. If it is true that these forms have assisted teachers in understanding or gaining knowledge about students, it is also true that many teachers have misused this information through prejudgment of the student and the tendency to stereotype students. Most of the latter actions have resulted from an improper understanding of the use and interpretation of data found on the cumulative record folder. If teachers are to utilize such information they can, with practice, increase their ability to use these forms and make this knowledge truly meaningful. More important than this, however, is the teacher's ability to sharpen her powers of observation. This is possible when the teacher:

1. realizes the necessity for careful, purposeful, and systematic observation;
2. realizes that steps should be taken to prevent stigmatic labels such as "dull child," or "problem child";

---

[15] Kaplan, *Mental Health and Human Relations in Education*, p. 317.

3. avoids a bias which favors one child over the group; and
4. learns to administer, score, and interpret standardized tests properly.

A technique which sometimes assists the teacher in gaining insight into the child's personality is the use of creative writing with a focus of attention upon such emotional topics as, "What I Feel About My Home" or "What I Feel When My Peer Group Forgets to Include Me." Frequently students may desire to respond to topics of their own choice. To encourage students to work toward such an objective not only permits them to write freely and to release tensions, but also serves to assist the teachers in gaining a better understanding of these students.

Teachers sometimes question the purpose of extended efforts to understand students. They feel, and perhaps rightly so, that the primary objective of the teacher is to impart skills and knowledge, and that when she has sufficient time to do anything other than this she will do what she can. Of the many statements made which were designed to assist teachers to understand the significance of the teacher-pupil relationship, it now seems that a composite or summary statement might best reflect the most vivid picture of what the results of such a relationship might logically be like. Naturally, such a summary statement would focus on the teacher-pupil relationship and would, essentially, attempt to answer specific questions. Within the confines of the information now available, it seems that the following questions and answers bring the challenge into proper perspective:

What have youngsters gained through experiences with teachers who have served as guidance workers and attempted to provide an atmosphere which nurtured the growth and development of their students? What can such teachers hope to accomplish through better teacher-pupil relations than has already been accomplished through more formal teacher-pupil relations?

First, they can hope to assist in the development of youngsters who, because of a good teacher-pupil relationship, have gained self-identity, i.e., the knowledge of who they are and how they can become contributors to the society of which they are a part.

Second, teachers can, through better teacher-pupil relations, assist youngsters to understand themselves as they function within the realm of stability when challenged by problems that might otherwise create for them feelings of frustration, anger, guilt, or fear. Then, too, teachers can ultimately provide for pupils the understanding which will assist them to remain tolerant, stable and well able to adapt to new situations because they know who they are and how they relate to the world around them.

Third, they can, through better teacher-pupil relations, assist youngsters not only to understand themselves better but to understand others better. Such understandings will, it seems, assist pupils to enter into relationships which are genuine and potentially reciprocal, i.e., relationships which will permit them to care about other people without being ashamed of their feelings or without feeling awkward in their relationships with others.

Fourth, improved relations with youngsters will assist them to reach a level of self-understanding which will permit them to become involved with other people because they are not constantly involved with themselves. Ultimately, they will reflect those characteristics of responsibility, self-respect, personal involvement, and respect for others which will magnify their potentials for contributing to the stability of society.

Fifth, through better teacher-pupil relations youngsters will be more capable of developing integrated and adequate concepts of themselves and how they relate to society—they will be able to test these concepts against the realities found in society and they will be able to convert these concepts into realities with satisfaction to themselves and benefit to society.

In essence, it might be said that these youngsters can experience, through such a relationship, the first in a series of steps leading to the maintenance and the enhancement of good mental health.

A resourceful teacher will undoubtedly be able to devise many new techniques to fit her own particular needs. Whatever these may be, the success of the guidance program will be largely in her hands and will, to a great extent, depend upon her ability to establish a good working relationship with each of the pupils.

7

PLACEMENT: A PATH TOWARD FULFILLMENT

One of the more noteworthy trends in recent years has been a gradual broadening of the school's conception of its responsibility for providing special types of placement assistance. Recognizing that students do not, of necessity, answer their placement needs when leaving school, it now appears that the trend is to provide services both for students in school and those who have left. This latter group may include former students who have dropped out of school prematurely or those who have graduated and seek proper placement as a path toward personal fulfillment. Naturally, there are both private and state supported agencies which provide professional placement services but interestingly enough, a guidance placement service is one of the few that can serve in both a coordinating capacity and a placement capacity. That is to say that when professional placement services are available, it may be well for the guidance placement service to serve as a liaison between the student and such a professional placement agency. A cooperative effort such as this provides a positive attitude toward the school and what it is attempting to do for its students.

A DUAL ROLE FOR PLACEMENT

Placement services that are sponsored within a school setting are designed not only to provide job placement but to assist students with special problems related to academic placement. This might include moving a student from one school to another or from one teacher to another, i.e., from English 101 with Miss Smith to English 101 with Mr. Ward. It might also include moving a student into a special type of educational experience such as Art 100 or Music 100 simply because such an experience may help him to develop a better personal sense of understanding about himself and how he relates to the world in which he lives.

Within such a framework, it seems essential to recognize how placement becomes a totally integrated part of the guidance program—that is, how it relates to other guidance services. Since placement involves the application of a variety of guidance services such as counseling, testing, group work, and the dissemination of information, it seems apparent that these services complement one another and that without a constellation of such services it would be difficult to establish an objective rationale for placing a student. On the other hand, without placement as a service, it is difficult to establish realistic objectives for that student—objectives which will serve as a motivating force throughout his academic career.

PLACEMENT COUNSELING: PITFALLS AND ADMONITIONS

As counselors become involved in the placement of students, it is often quite easy for them to forget that one of their primary responsibilities is to assist individuals to grow in their capacity to be responsible and self-sufficient. Although the student may have an immediate need for a job or to select a college, ultimately he will be confronted with a continuing responsibility for making decisions relative to the development of a lifelong career. This means that counselors must concern themselves with a student's long-range objective of personal development while attending to his immediate objective of getting a job or selecting a college.

As an example of the problem involved, Joe Smith may initially seek a job which is consistent with his present needs for financial support and with his current view of self in terms of what he is and what he has to offer. However, as he gains experience and maturity, he will probably begin to see himself in a different light, will become dissatisfied with his initial choice, and will eventually seek another position which more nearly meets his changing needs. On the average, Joe can be expected to change occupations at least three to four times during his life span in an evolving pattern of career development.

Thus, if the placement service is to assist Joe adequately in meeting his vocational needs, he must learn in his initial placement experiences the skills and insights which he will need subsequently to plan and carry out his lifelong pattern of career development. In this sense, placement is not something to be done for Joe so much as it is something which helps him to learn to do for himself. It seems that we are becoming more and more aware of the fact that securing a suitable job or selecting an appropriate academic institution is only one part of a total learning experience the nature of which is defined in terms of a process rather than a product—a means to an end rather than the end itself.

INVOLVING STUDENTS

There is, it seems, much to be said for involving students directly in various aspects of placement and especially for the technique of learning about jobs through well-planned occupational surveys conducted by students. Through such surveys students are encouraged to contact employers or personnel men with whom the guidance counselor has previously arranged appointments. From such an experience students learn about employment settings, about collecting information relative to these settings, and about the proper utilization of such information as a means of bringing satisfaction to themselves and benefit to society.

A word of caution at this point: if the survey is to be successful, it is extremely important to remember that appointments for occupational surveys must always be arranged well in advance by the guidance counselor and that once granted such an appointment the student's relationship with the potential employer is governed by a well-structured questionnaire designed specifically to get the information most essential to the objectives of the survey.

Since placement, by nature, is most appropriately concerned with the development and utilization of human resources, much can be said for a team approach in making a "good" placement service a reality. If such an assumption is correct, at least to the extent to which it now appears to be correct, then the success of a placement service will have much to do with the approach used by the team, by the attitude of the team members toward students, and by the ability of the team to provide positive and meaningful placement experiences for students who need such experiences.

Given proper administrative support, it now seems that the dimensions of a placement service within a school setting have few limitations. However, some school situations do impose practical limitations on the scope of such a service. Recognizing these limitations is, of course, one of the responsibilities of the counselor and soon alerts him to the fact that he cannot be all things to all people but rather must determine in what ways he can best serve each individual.

A FUNCTIONAL APPROACH TO PLACEMENT

Utilizing a team approach to placement is never simple. The first and perhaps most challenging responsibility of the counselor in this respect is to attempt to determine who among the many people available can most logically serve as team members. In this particular type of setting, it appears that members of the team might most appropriately be individuals who are industrialists, state employment counselors, religious leaders, vocational rehabilitation counselors, employers, teachers, school administrators, and all other people who may be significant in the placement of a student.

The functions to be incorporated into the placement program

of a school system will always be determined by such unique characteristics as the background and training of those who are in charge of the placement service, the level of financial support provided for such a service, the recognition of a need for such a service, and the cooperative efforts of team members to coordinate such a service. Perhaps the following list of functions might serve to clarify and define those things which will serve as a focus of attention when implementing a placement service.

Educational Placement

1. Through counseling, students are exposed to alternative educational choice patterns made possible through identifying their strengths and establishing tentative goals in terms of their interests, abilities, aspirations, special aptitudes, and personality characteristics.

2. Up-to-date information about educational programs is collected, organized and made available to students who are interested in exploring such information.

3. Arrangements are made for representatives of accredited educational institutions such as colleges and universities to visit the school setting periodically in order to discuss their respective programs with interested students and parents.

4. A systematic check is made to make sure that all educational institutions to which students are referred are accredited institutions.

Job Placement

1. Through counseling, students are given assistance in exploring various job opportunities and in making decisions relative to vocational choices.

2. Up-to-date information about job opportunities in the community as well as descriptive information about employers is collected, organized, and made avaliable to students.

3. Suggestions and information regarding recommended procedures and practices for seeking a job are shared with students through publications, individual counseling and group guidance sessions.

4. Avenues of communication between the school and potential employers are developed and maintained in order to facilitate contacts by students.

5. Close liaison is maintained between the school placement program and community agencies which provide vocational or employment services thus providing students with a broader exploitation of the many avenues of assistance open to them.

6. Placement files are initiated and maintained for all students seeking employment. Copies of the files are made available to employers who may potentially hire students.

7. Where feasible and desirable, arrangements are made whereby personnel people of major employers in the community may interview student applicants at the school.

8. Arrangements are made for students, individually or in groups, to visit employment settings they are considering.

Services to Employers

1. Employers are given assistance in finding suitable applicants for position vacancies.

2. The placement program serves as a liaison between the school and employers in the community. Through lines of communication with the placement service, employers are more able to make their needs known to the school system.

Services to Other Educational Institutions

1. The channels of communication between the counselor and other educational institutions such as trade schools, colleges, and universities assist admissions personnel in making requirements and special features of their respective programs known to applicants.

2. The counselor becomes a contact person through whom other educational institutions may obtain special types of information about students applying for admission to their programs.

Services to a School

1. The placement of former students into appropriate jobs or educational settings enables a school to show tangible results of its program.

2. Through reciprocal relationships established between the placement service and employers, community agencies, and other educational institutions, a school has direct access to key segments of the community-at-large.

3. Through continued assistance provided to former students and through follow-up studies of school leavers, a school is able to obtain up-to-date information on the developmental progress of former students. Such information may be used by the school in evaluating its program.

4. The screening, selection and placement of students into special programs within the school assists the administration and faculty in implementing various curricular decisions.

COORDINATING YOUR EFFORTS WITH COMMUNITY AGENCIES

The school placement program can do much to increase its overall effectiveness, especially with vocational placement, through cooperating with community agencies having parallel functions. While there will always be some overlap in services offered, most of these agencies provide special features in their services which, if coordinated properly with the school program, can do much to broaden the scope of placement services available in the community.

One of the initial steps in achieving such coordination is to visit with key agency officials in order to establish a basis for harmonious relationships and to discuss ways in which the respective programs can be made to work together in a mutually beneficial way. The counselors may find it beneficial to concentrate on special testing programs administered by the agency, special types of information which might be available through that particular agency, and special entry and preparatory programs which the agency might administer as a means of assisting individuals to enter particular fields of work.

Quite often, agency officials are willing to serve the school placement service in an auxiliary capacity. This is especially true if the school placement service is designed to increase the flexibility of the private placement service as students are moved into a community-oriented situation. For example, agencies will often supply resource people when students need special types of information. On other occasions, they will supply skilled personnel to administer special test batteries to groups of students who are about to enter the world of work or to provide services which are generally supportive of, and complementary to, the school placement program.

The presence of agencies having placement-related functions in any given community is, of course, always dependent on factors such as the size of the community and the need for such services. Even though some of these agencies do not have branches in the community proper, they are usually willing to extend assistance on request. As an illustration of what might be done, one has only to look at some of these agencies and the services they provide.

The State Employment Service

The state employment service operates branch offices in most of the major cities and communities within each state. Affiliated with the United States Employment Service, this state agency offers a variety of placement services which are geared to meeting the widely varying needs of the general public. Services of interest to school counselors, typically included in their operations, are: (1) administration of the U.S. Employment Service's General Aptitude Test Battery (GATB) which may be useful as a counseling aid; (2) specific information about job vacancies locally and elsewhere; (3) trends and developments in the labor market; (4) information about local and state employers; and (5) employment counseling from trained agency personnel.

Private Employment Agencies

Most communities of any size have one or more employment agencies which provide services on some type of fee arrangement. While in certain critical fields, these fees may be paid by the employer it is a more common practice for the applicant to pay the cost of services. Arrangements typically involve payment of a set percentage of salary or wages over a given period of time.

Placement services provided by the private agencies will often be oriented to a particular clientele since they usually are able to develop a better program by staying within a narrow field of specialties. Unless such agencies are regulated by the state, the quality of service provided may vary considerably from one to the next. In general, school counselors should check them out thoroughly before making referrals.

The private agency may, in some instances, provide a more individualized, more intensive type of assistance than that available from non-fee agencies. However, students should probably be advised to explore fully nonprofit avenues of assistance before seeking placement assistance with this type of agency.

State Vocational Rehabilitation Service

The state operated Vocational Rehabilitation Service offers placement assistance for special categories of students who can qualify for their services. This typically includes students affected by various types of physical and emotional disabilities. Counselors within each state should become aware of the specific requirements for obtaining assistance under this type of program.

Not only do counselors working with the rehabilitation services provide personal counseling for their clients, but they often go beyond the capabilities of most school counselors in facilitating various aspects of adjustment. In many instances clients are provided special types of assistance geared to the individual needs for making adjustment to a job or in attending a training program.

Veterans Administration Counseling Program

Under provisions of federal legislation, the Veterans Administration provides special benefits to dependents of veterans who are deceased or who are totally and permanently disabled. This program primarily provides assistance to dependents who plan to enroll in various types of training and preparatory experiences. Services typically include testing, individual counseling, and the provision of educational-vocational information. The closest office of the Veterans Administration can usually provide preliminary information.

Apprenticeship Program

There are a number of groups and agencies which administer or coordinate various types of apprenticeship or on-the-job training programs as a means of facilitating the entry of individuals into various occupational specialties. Labor unions often utilize some type of apprenticeship as an entry vehicle for new members having little or no training in their fields. Not to be overlooked are work-study programs which may be operated in conjunction with vocational programs in the secondary school itself or in nearby junior colleges or technical institutes. It is usually desirable to obtain specific information about requirements and opportunities from program representatives.

Church Sponsored Guidance Programs

One of the more recent trends in the area of vocational guidance is more widespread sponsorship of various guidance-oriented activities by major religious groups. Two of the more notable examples are the Presbyterian Guidance Program and the Jewish B'nai B'rith Vocational Service.* One of the unique features of these programs is that they often utilize the services of interested lay people working under the supervision of trained guidance workers. Activities sponsored by them include such things as precounseling orientation, provision of vocational information, testing, and personal counseling. Pastors and key members of these organizations can usually supply details and information about their programs.

Selecting an Appropriate Agency

The selection of an appropriate agency when assistance of some type seems desirable is the key element in the success or

---

* Note: Materials may be obtained from Board of Christian Education, Box 1176, Richmond, Virginia 23209, and B'nai B'rith Vocational Service Bureau, 1761 R. Street, NW, Washington, D.C. 20549.

failure of cooperation with community agencies. The first considerations should be the type of special assistance needed and the potential of the particular agencies under consideration to meet the needs of students. Other factors such as the proximity of an agency office, the kind of working relationship existing between the agency and the school placement program, and the availability of agency personnel should then be important factors in determining the direction in which assistance will be sought. As a means of helping counselors to identify as quickly as possible sources of assistance, Table 1 provides a summary of some more prominent community agencies and the related services they may make available to students.

UNDERSTANDING THE EXPECTANCY GAP

Although the placement of students both within and outside of the school setting is of great importance, of even greater importance to students is a team effort on the part of counselors, teachers, administrators and parents to close what might logically be referred to as the "Expectancy Gap." [1] That is, to close the gap between what students expect to find in projected new situations and, conversely, what will be expected of them in return.

As a person who seeks employment, for example, the student's main concern at the moment he contacts the prospective employer involves the total work climate which encompasses the job for which he plans to apply. It can be assumed that much of what he expects will be a reflection of his experiential syndrome, i.e., all those past experiences which have contributed to his present existence. Many of these expectations were, perhaps, ideas that were originally introduced through his relationship with his family, his teachers or other significant persons in his life. So deeply are the imprints of these experiences imbedded

---

[1] K. U. Gutsch et al. "Counseling: Understanding the Expectancy Gap," *Journal of Employment Counseling*, Vol. V, No. 3 (September, 1968), pp. 92–94.

TABLE 1

SERVICES PROVIDED THROUGH COMMUNITY AGENCIES

SERVICE	AGENCY	WHAT IS DONE	HOW TO CONTACT AGENCY
Vocational Rehabilitation	Veteran's Administration [1]	Testing and evaluation Counseling Dissemination of occupational information Placement & job follow-up Maintenance provided during training Physical rehabilitation assisted through artificial limbs, hearing aids, etc.	[1] Local Veterans Service Office or State Employment Service for information.
	State Vocational Rehabilitation Service [2]		[2] Local Office or contact Welfare Department for information.
Employment and Job Placement Counseling	State Employment Service [3]	Testing and evaluation Employment counseling Dissemination of occupational information Job placement & follow-up	[3] Offices located in major cities and county or parish seats.
	Private Employment Agencies [4]		[4] Telephone Directory for local offices or branches.

Vocational Exploration and Career Counseling	Church-related Guidance Programs [5] Veteran's Administration [1]	Precounseling orientation Testing and evaluation Dissemination of vocational information Vocational and career counseling	[5] Pastor or lay leaders of local churches and especially Presbyterian churches. [6] Local Chamber Office.
Information about Trends and Projections in Labor Market	State Employment Service [3] Chamber of Commerce [6] State Research & Development Agency [7]	Research concerning development of new labor markets Dissemination of current information about trends and developments in local and regional labor markets through publications, newsletters, and resource speakers	[7] Director of State Offices or contact Chamber of Commerce for information. [8] Telephone Directory for local union in appropriate field.
Apprenticeship Programs and Work-Study Programs	State Employment Service [3] Labor Unions [8] H. S. Vocational Programs [9]	Placement and follow-up in entry apprenticeship programs	[9] Local School System.

in his mind that the values which emerge cause him to expect certain things from his employer. It is this expectation which sometimes leads him into a relationship of dissonance with his employer especially if these expectations differ significantly from the corresponding expectations of the employer.

Within the confines of such relationships, it seems obvious that there is a strong desire for reciprocity. It appears that employers tend to be more concerned with factors such as absenteeism, on-the-job conduct, production, licensing, and enforcement policies while employees are more concerned with salaries, work conditions, paid holidays, and occupational mobility, i.e., the opportunity to advance while on the job. Naturally to move from the present setting into a new one is both interesting and challenging. Yet, for those students who fail to understand the complexity of the transition, continued failures create for them a special type of feeling about themselves. Perhaps they realize for the first time that they have only minimal contributions which they can make to gain the societal respect they would like to have. Ultimately, prolonged exposure to such conditions destroys the very fabric of their existence and nurtures within them a seed of dissent.

Thus, if we can recognize the expectancy gap as an important factor in the establishment of better relationships among students and those who will be responsible for their management and supervision in future educational-vocational settings, it may be possible to work out a method of operation which will assist the potential employee or continuing student to make the transition with a much better sense of understanding and direction. Such an impetus would call for greater sophistication on the part of our placement services than we now have. Then, too, it would call for a more comprehensive understanding of students, a better understanding of those settings into which they expect to move, and a continued search for better and more innovative placement procedures. As a result of such an emphasis, students would, perhaps, realize a greater feeling of stability when initiating contacts relative to making a transition and ultimately reflect greater security in their decision making.

CLOSING THE EXPECTANCY GAP

With the emphasis in recent years on continued training and preparation beyond the secondary school, a major task of school counselors has been that of assisting college-bound graduates to make appropriate selections among the many institutions of higher learning. As admission's requirements have become increasingly restrictive, students have needed more accurate information about applicant requirements and the descriptive characteristics of institutions under consideration.

One of the major shortcomings of the descriptive materials typically distributed by colleges and universities has been the general lack of information which lends itself to comparisons. Consequently many youngsters have chosen programs because of vague expectations about the nature and quality of course offerings and the general climate of the campus. In many cases, these expectations have not been borne out by subsequent experiences.

As counselors attempt to close the expectancy gap for students going on for further education, it is important that they be provided with descriptive information which will enable them to make realistic comparisons among possible choices. Using the catalogues and bulletins of the institutions as an informational base, the counselor should move beyond these sources to other types of materials which will point up the uniqueness of particular institutions and their respective programs.

Explorations for such information would logically begin with the student and his personal plans for further study. Having entered into a process of self-examination and exploration prior to seeking placement assistance, students should be ready to look at the range of programs meeting their somewhat crystallized educational needs. Beyond their needs for particular types of academic experiences, they should be interested in other aspects of the campus environment which may potentially contribute to their personal satisfaction and success.

As a preliminary step in narrowing the field, students might be directed to one of the standard guides to educational institutions such as *New American Guide to Colleges*[2] or *Lovejoy's Vocational School Guide*.[3] These references group institutions by states and provide brief descriptive information about the institutions with respect to student body, faculty, courses and degrees offered, financial aids available, admissions requirements and procedures, and enrollment figures. With this information, the student can quickly compare training institutions within the geographic area of his choice.

In examining literature relative to such institutions, students may then be interested in other identifying characteristics. Researchers such as C. R. Pace and G. G. Stern[4] have developed techniques for assessing and profiling the psychological characteristics of various college environments. One of the more potentially useful approaches recently developed has been the Environmental Assessment Technique.[5] After applying the EAS at 248 colleges and universities, Astin published the results in a form which may be easily profiled, thereby making the data of use to counselors in comparing the characteristics of institutions and their entering freshman classes.

Once the student has narrowed the field to a small number of institutions, it is usually a good idea to arrange for him to talk with admissions representatives from each school. This may be accomplished either through a visit to the campus or by inviting representatives from the institutions to your school. The on-campus visit has the advantages of allowing the student to see the campus firsthand and to talk with faculty members and students, thereby gaining a more definite impression of what respective institutions are really like.

---

[2] G. R. Hawes, *New American Guide to Colleges* (3rd ed.; New York: Columbia University Press, 1966).

[3] C. E. Lovejoy, *Lovejoy's Vocational School Guide* (New York: Simon and Schuster, 1963).

[4] C. R. Pace and G. G. Stern, "An Approach to the Measurement of Psychological Characteristics of College Environments," *Journal of Educational Psychology* (October 1958), pp. 269–77.

[5] A. W. Astin, *Who Goes Where to College?* (Chicago: Science Research Associates, Inc., 1965).

Providing Job Opportunity Information

The provision of accurate job opportunity information is a major facet of an effective placement service. While commercially produced occupational information kits are useful, they are general in nature and often do not answer many of the questions which arise in relation to specific job opportunities in the local community. Thus, if the counselor is to provide an adequate source of information, he must also gain up-to-date information about the local employers who provide work opportunities for his students.

Since this more specific information is not available from the commercial suppliers, the counselor must take the initiative in gathering data needed by his students. The counselor should, in general, select methods which seem appropriate for his situation. The "Jobs for Youth" program of the Newton, Massachusetts, public schools provides an excellent example of how such an activity might be carried out in a comprehensive career development program. The guidelines for the project, *Career Information Service,* provide a complete outline of procedures and forms used by the Newton program.[6] The following specific ideas are offered here as examples of activities which might be implemented in most school situations. They offer advantages in terms of simplicity of operation, little or no direct costs, direct involvement of students, and the generation of good public relations in the community as a side effect.

A Community Occupational Survey—As mentioned at the beginning of this chapter, one of the more effective means of initiating contacts with employers and gathering job opportunity information is the community occupational survey. In this approach, students make personal contacts with employer officials as a means of getting, firsthand, up-to-date information about the company, the kind of job opportunities available now and

---

[6] D. F. Circle, D. B. Clemens, A. M. Kroll, and D. C. Overholt, *Career Information Service* (Commonwealth of Massachusetts: Bureau of Vocational Education, Department of Education, 1968), pp. 39–80.

anticipated in the future, and the general working conditions. During this survey contact, employers should be encouraged to file continually vacancy information with the school placement service. This type of activity may often be initiated as a class project or a special project for student groups such as the student government association.

While there are any number of directories which may be used as a means of lining up contacts for students, the yellow pages of the telephone book usually will provide one of the most complete and readily accessible sources for planning your survey. Once the list of firms to be contacted has been compiled, it may be further checked and revised using other listings such as Chamber of Commerce Directory and the city directory. Each source will be surveyed to determine what jobs are available for dropouts and for graduates. Information of importance will include such things as job description, starting wage, potential for advancement, occupational hazards, fringe benefits, and educational and experiential requirements for entering the field.

One of the key ingredients in the successful community survey is preplanning. Not only should groundwork be laid with employers to be contacted, but students making the contacts should be briefed and given instructions. In order to publicize the survey and set the stage for student interviews, the placement service should contact the employers by letter explaining the purposes of the program. In addition, it may be helpful in larger communities to alert the public to the coming survey through the news media and through contacts with key organizations such as civic clubs and the Chamber of Commerce.

In working with the students who will be conducting the survey, it is usually appropriate to define their role in relation to the survey, emphasizing the importance of establishing good relationships which will keep the program moving in the future. It may be desirable to supply the students with some type of survey guide to insure that complete information will be gained in every case. The following areas might be included in a job opportunity survey guide:

1. General Information—Name of firm; name of representa-

tive to be contacted when applying for a job; address; phone number.

2. Type of Business or Industry—Kinds of products; local or national operation, and the like.

3. Vacancy Information—Number of positions; duties; applicant qualifications; working conditions; duration of position and opportunities for advancement.

Once the information is collected, it should be compiled and summarized in a form which will facilitate its use by students. The employer information should be used to cultivate and further develop close working relationships with employers in the community.

A Follow-up Study—The follow-up study, described in greater detail in Chapter 8, not only supplies valuable data for the evaluation of the school program, but potentially may be very useful as a means of collecting job opportunity information. Since the follow-up study is designed to focus primarily on those students who have left school, it may be used to identify employers and the kind of jobs that they have generally made available to students. The follow-up study might logically be structured to identify major problems encountered by students seeking positions, thereby providing guidelines for improving the placement service.

The follow-up study is perhaps most effective when it is conducted on a periodic basis. In this way, it provides a much more adequate reflection of trends in job opportunities in the community and it helps the school to follow the career development of former students. As a general rule it would seem desirable to conduct follow-up studies at the end of the first year of employment for recent leavers and at least every five years for all former students.

A Postcard Approach—In some cases, funds may not be available for the purchase of a good occupational information subscription service, especially when a guidance program is first initiated. Since some type of general informational file seems essential for vocational exploration, the counselor may want to develop a suitable file from other sources. Such a file can fill the needs of students until a subscription can be obtained, and it may be useful as a supplement afterward.

One of the simplest approaches to developing such a file is to request printed information from various organizations which make occupational monographs available—many of them at no cost. If funds are a problem, the postcard usually is an adequate medium for making the request.

Since this activity essentially involves communication skills, it is often possible to enlist the assistance of students in one of the instructional areas. A listing of occupational literature such as G. Forrester's annotated bibliography of occupational literature will provide a basic source from which to identify materials to be requested as well as the supplying organizations.[7] If it seems desirable to limit the scope of the file, the counselor may want to survey the student body to determine which occupational areas are of interest to them and then to ask only for monographs covering these areas. Once the file is established, the file may be continually expanded to meet the needs of students.

Getting the Word to Employers

Providing information for the expectancy gap is a two-sided coin. To be sure, it is important to provide information about job opportunities for students. It is equally important that employers in the community be furnished with pertinent information about students who will be available for employment. In this way the expectancy gap may be effectively closed with students and employers alike becoming more fully aware of resources that are available to them in meeting their respective needs.

A Placement File—It is often helpful to employers for the placement service to furnish some type of information about placement registrants at their request. Such information would logically be collected on job application forms completed by students when they register with the placement service. Typically these forms contain basic descriptive information, educational

---

[7] G. Forrester, *Occupational Literature* (New York: H. W. Wilson, 1964).

background information, work experience, and references to be contacted. The job application form included as Figure 7–1 provides a good format which is efficient yet adequate in terms of information contained on it.

Placed in a file, these completed application forms provide a ready source of information about registrants which may be easily made available to employers enabling them to obtain preliminary information for the evaluation of applicants. It also provides a working file for the counselor who attempts to bring employers and prospective employees together. Once the student is employed, his file may be placed on an inactive status until such time as he seeks another position. Since the placement file should be continuously updated, it provides a valuable reservoir of information about the student's career development.

A Placement Registrant Bulletin—It is often desirable for the placement service to initiate procedures which bring students to the attention of employers, especially in larger communities. Some type of placement registrant bulletin may be useful for this purpose since it can be mailed to all possible employers allowing them to see who is available to meet their employment needs. Not only does the bulletin have the advantage of bringing current placement registrants to the attention of employers, but it also helps to develop contacts which may generate other opportunities in the future.

There are several approaches which may be effectively utilized in developing placement registrant bulletins. Along more simple lines, the bulletin may contain only a brief paragraph about each registrant listing the descriptive information as shown in the following example:

> Joe J. Smith. Desires position as carpenter's apprentice. Received H. S. Diploma May, 1968. 2 years experience, afternoons and summers, with local millwork firm. Single, Age 17, Excellent health, No physical disabilities. Desires location within 50-mile radius.

To improve the utility of the bulletin for employers, the registrant listings should be grouped according to type of position desired.

JOB APPLICATION
(Please type or print neatly)

Name _____
    (Last)   (Middle)   (First)

Address _____
    (Street No.)   (City & State)

Date of Birth _____
    (mo.)   (day)   (yr.)

Physical Disabilities: yes ___ no ___
If yes, specify below.

_____

Type of Work wanted: _____

Hrs. per week: _____
Reason for wanting job: _____

Date available: _____
Driver's License? yes ___ no ___
Car available? yes ___ no ___

Date _____
Phone _____
Grade now in _____

DO NOT WRITE HERE

Counselor _____
Vocational Goals: ___
_____
Comments: _____
_____

Times available for work:
Mon. _____
Tue. _____
Wed. _____
Thur. _____
Fri. _____
Sat. _____
Sun. _____

School courses which help to qualify you for work: _____

Honors: _____
Hobbies: _____
Extracurricular activities: _____

Referrals

(Date) (Employer) (Results)

WORK EXPERIENCES

(Period of Employment) (Employer) (Address) (Type of Work Performed)

REFERENCES

(Name) (Address) (Relationship to Applicant)

_____ _____
Applicant's Signature   Parent's Approval Signature

Figure 7-1

Subsequent bulletins would be used to update the previous lists of registrants and to pass along information which may be of interest to the employer.

A Personal Data Brochure—In some cases it is desirable to share more information with employers than is possible with the placement registrant bulletin. This may be true, for example, when assisting students who have gone through special vocational-technical programs or when working with adults who have had a more extensive background of qualifying experience than is normally the case with regular students. This procedure essentially calls for the development of personal data sheets for each student similar to the example shown in Figure 7–2. These data sheets are then reproduced in multiple copies, assembled into brochures, and distributed to prospective employers. When working with large numbers of students, it is usually wise to develop separate brochures for students in each major employment category.

CONTACTING EMPLOYERS

Once the good job prospects have been identified, the next step is to make the initial contact with the employer. If employers do not come to the school placement office for interviews, the student must contact them in their own settings. Usually the employer should be contacted either through a visit to his personnel office or by letter if the employer is located some distance away or if the number of employers being contacted is too large to make visits to all feasible. In this way, the letter of application serves to narrow the field to those who are really good prospects.

In general, letters of application should be directed to specific job vacancies which have been identified in the job opportunity information collected by the placement service. This helps the employer to place the application in a particular context which lends itself to a more favorable evaluation.

The purpose of the letter of application is to introduce the candidate to the employer and to indicate how his qualifications relate favorably to the requirements of the position or positions

SAMPLE PERSONAL DATA SHEET

Name: Joe J. Smith

Permanent Address: 2011 10th Ave. Central City

Marital Status: single

Available: Immediately

photo (optional)

Phone: 266-7211

Health: Excellent, no disabilities

Career Objectives
Would like to become master carpenter, possibly becoming construction foreman at some later time.

Education
H. S. Diploma, Central City High School, May, 1970

Note: Took special vocational courses in woodworking and blueprint reading as electives during last two years of high school. Plan to continue training at night in vocational-technical program of county jr. college.

Work Experience
1966–present—Helper, Norton Millwork Co., Central City.
1964–66—Delivery Boy, Central City Newspaper

Military Status
Currently fulfilling military obligation as member of Army National Guard. Rank, Cpl.

References
Ralph F. Jones, Counselor, Central City High School
William A. Smith, Route Mgr., Central City News
Ronald Norton, Owner, Norton Millwork Co., Central City

Note: Additional information may be obtained on request from Central City High School Placement Office.

Figure 7–2

desired. Figure 7–3 provides a guide which may be used to develop a letter of application. As an enclosure to the letter, it is usually a good idea to attach a personal data sheet similar to that shown in Figure 7–2. This is especially true when the applicant has special training and/or extensive experiences which relate to his application.

WHAT TO EXPECT DURING THE EMPLOYMENT INTERVIEW

After preliminary contact has been made with prospective employers and application procedures have been completed, applicants will usually be asked to come for interviews if they indicate promise for employment. In helping students to put their best foot forward, counselors might suggest that they be on time and be appropriately dressed. In the interview, the employer is usually interested in obtaining more knowledge of the applicant than was contained in his initial application. The interviewer will usually attempt to gain rather subjective impressions about the appearance of the applicant, his reliability and integrity, his speech and manners, his reasons for making application, and his qualifications for positions which may be available.

Students should be helped to realize that the employment interview is a two-way street, i.e., there is a reciprocity involved in which the interviewer attempts to answer questions about the desirability of employing the applicant while the applicant, in turn, attempts to determine if the employer really has something worthwhile to offer. Thus, the applicant potentially has as much to gain from the interview as the employer. In general, students should attempt to answer questions in a genuine and straightforward manner. They should ask questions which will gain the information they need in order to evaluate employment opportunities offered by the employer.

Before going for the interview, it is often advisable for the applicant to become familiar with the prospective employer and his operation. If this knowledge is coupled with an adequate amount of self-understanding in terms of assets to be offered and work objectives to be sought, the applicant is then in a much better position to interact in the employment interview.

SUGGESTED STYLE FOR APPLICATION LETTER
AND FORMULA FOR CONTENT *

2010 10th Ave.
Central City, USA
July 2, 1968

Mr. George McCormick
Director of Personnel
American Construction Co.
124 South Third Street
Central City, USA

Dear Mr. McCormick:

Opening Paragraph: State why you are writing, name the position or type of work for which you are applying, and mention how you heard of the opening.

Middle Paragraphs: Explain why you are interested in working for this employer and specify your reasons for desiring this type of work. If you have had experience, be sure to point out your particular achievements or other qualifications in this field or type of work. Refer the reader to the attached application blank or personal data sheet, or whatever media you are using to illustrate your training, interests, and experiences.

Closing Paragraph: Have an appropriate closing to pave the way for the interview by asking for an appointment, by giving your phone number, or by offering some similar suggestion to facilitate an immediate and favorable reply. Ending your letter with a question encourages a reply.

Very truly yours,
Joe J. Smith

Enclosure

Figure 7–3

* Adapted by permission from Robert Calvert, Jr., and John E. Steele, *Planning Your Career* (New York: McGraw-Hill Book Co., Inc., 1965.)

USING DATA PROCESSING IN PLACEMENT

With the large volume of data and materials to be processed in educational systems, many schools have installed data processing equipment in order to cut down on time required by professional staff in handling many of the routine clerical tasks. In addition to the increased speed in processing data, this equipment offers the advantage of increased accuracy in that most data processing systems include self-checking devices.

Where a data processing system has been installed by a school, the placement service may use this equipment to great advantage. For counselors desiring assistance in incorporating automatic data processing procedures into their program, a detailed guide is available from the Automated Education Center.[8]

IMPLEMENTING THE PLACEMENT SERVICE

Ideas and innovations such as those presented in this chapter are of little value unless they can be effectively put to work within the context of the guidance program as it exists in each school. The introduction of any procedure must, of necessity, be preceded by an adequate amount of planning. Such planning logically starts with the objectives of the school's placement program and proceeds to the careful consideration of techniques and procedures which will best move that program toward the attainment of its objectives. In this way, the placement program becomes more nearly tailor-made for the school and the surrounding community. The actual content of the placement program thus reflects, to a great extent, the uniqueness of the school.

If the introduction of new procedures represents drastic changes in the existing program, steps should be taken to insure the smoothest transition possible. Transition can usually be improved through supplying up-to-date information about the changes to students, employers and other school personnel;

---

[8] G. E. Pierce, *Data Processing for Guidance and Counseling* (Detroit, Michigan: Box 2658, Automated Education Center, 1967).

through coordination with agencies and employers affected by the changes; and, where possible, through direct involvement of other school personnel, employers and students in the consideration of possible changes to be initiated.

8

EVALUATING YOUR RESULTS: SOME INNOVATIONS THROUGH RESEARCH

Of vital importance to change and improvement in guidance and counseling is the evaluation of program outcomes. While the guidance program is by its very nature difficult to evaluate, many of the problems which are typically encountered may be overcome if counselors adequately understand the process of evaluation and are able to translate this understanding into action through workable ideas and innovations.

WHY EVALUATE?

If guidance workers are to improve their program it seems that they must have at their disposal suitable procedures for studying their program and making value judgments about various guidance services. Since any program of worth must always operate in relation to certain objectives, regardless of how vaguely defined they might be, the information gained through evaluation allows the counselor to determine more rationally the extent to which his program is moving toward specific goals.

The information gained through the evaluative process may be used for a number of specific purposes which are important to the success of a guidance program:

1. To determine the extent to which the guidance program is, in fact, meeting the needs of the various school and community groups it attempts to serve.
2. To determine how well the guidance program is actually accomplishing its stated objectives.
3. To determine the extent to which students are utilizing the services that are being offered.
4. To check the validity of underlying assumptions and hypotheses on which objectives of the program are based.
5. To serve as a rational basis for making changes and revisions in the program.
6. To provide factual support for budgetary requests needed for further development of the program.
7. To provide objective information which may be used by the school in reporting to the community on the status and effectiveness of its programs.

CHARACTERISTICS OF A GOOD EVALUATION PROGRAM

While there are a number of important features in a good evaluation program, the following might serve to identify some of the more salient characteristics to be desired.

1. The program of evaluation should be comprehensive in scope and should not leave gaps in the information needed to evaluate the overall effectiveness of the guidance program.
2. Evaluation should be a continuous, ongoing process which serves as a beginning for change and improvement rather than as an end in itself.
3. Provisions are always made for interpretation and possible application of research findings as a follow-up to evaluative procedures.
4. The evaluation of the guidance program should proceed with a sense of relationship to the total school program.
5. The processes of evaluation should be worked into the

normal school procedures as routinely as possible in order to reduce the special effect such activities might have on students, faculty members, and others as well as to minimize disruption of normal activities.
6. Whenever possible, behavioral changes should provide one of the major categories of data to be used in determining the effect of the guidance program on student growth and development. The focus should be on changes in measurable behavior patterns which are relevant to the specific objectives being evaluated.
7. While the evaluation should always involve the total guidance staff, it should also include the widest possible staff participation from other areas of the school.

THREE KEY STEPS IN EVALUATION

The process of evaluation involves three basic tasks: (a) defining the objectives of the program in meaningful terms, (b) developing criteria or "yardsticks" which may be used to gauge the degree to which objectives are attained, and (c) taking measurements of the program which may then be analyzed in terms of the criteria. By approaching these tasks in this order, the evaluation process becomes more logical, and data obtained lends itself to a more meaningful interpretation.

Defining Objectives

While most guidance workers readily give lip service to certain objectives, they seldom take the time and trouble to spell out these objectives. However, as the initial step in the evaluative process, these objectives must be clearly identified so that they may be easily translated into expected outcomes. If the objectives of the program are stated in broad general terms, there remains the task of breaking down these more general statements into the specific behavioral outcomes that are desired.

Even though a list of general objectives may be provided in the school's statement of philosophy, it is usually necessary for the guidance staff to develop a more definitive list. In so doing, staff members should keep in mind the fact that the guidance program does not operate in a vacuum, but is an integral part of the school's total program. It is within this context that the guidance program's unique objectives take on their most important meaning. Therefore, the objectives of the guidance program must be developed in the light of the broader objectives of the school system.

Developing "Yardsticks"

Once the guidance staff has clarified and specified its program objectives, it then becomes necessary to develop criteria which serve as "yardsticks" of program achievement. In a sense, the counselor is concerned at this point with selecting standards against which measurements of program outcomes may be checked as evidence of attainment or nonattainment of stated objectives.

One objective of the guidance program, for example, may be to improve in-school adjustment of students. In evaluating the extent to which this objective has been attained, the counselor might use operational criteria such as trends in the school dropout rate, the incidence of disciplinary problems, and the number of curriculum changes. In order to get a picture which is complete, it is desirable to use a wide range of criteria.

A rather comprehensive attempt at developing such a yardstick is illustrated by Georgia Sachs as twenty-seven criteria were utilized under the following eight major areas in an effort to evaluate group guidance: (a) Adjustment to School, (b) Adjustment in Social Relationships, (c) Personal or Self-Adjustment, (d) Self-Appraisal, (e) Information Basic to Life Planning, (f) Teacher-Pupil Relationships, (g) Evaluative Reactions of Teachers and Pupils and (h) Effectiveness of Life Planning.[1]

Employing Measures

Having determined what the "yardsticks" for evaluation are to be, measurements must then be made to determine what move-

---

[1] Georgia M. Sachs in Percival W. Hutson, *The Guidance Function in Education* (2nd ed.; New York: Appleton-Century-Crofts, Educational Division, Meredith Corporation, 1968), pp. 770–71.

ment, if any, is being made toward stated objectives. At this point, the counselor is concerned with developing and employing assessment procedures which will gather the evidence needed to judge the adequacy of the program. If the evidence obtained is to lend itself to proper interpretation, the selection of instruments and procedures employed must proceed from the objectives to be evaluated.

As has been implied, greatest consideration must be given to selecting the approaches used for evaluating the guidance program. If the appraisal is to be from an external frame of reference, the criteria will have to be selected on the basis of services now being offered. If, on the other hand, the appraisal is to be from an internal frame of reference, it will have to include attitudes of clients, faculty members, and parents and their opinions and feelings about the guidance services.

DEVELOPING THE EVALUATION MASTER PLAN

In evaluating the guidance program, it is usually wise to engage in some amount of preplanning. One procedure which helps to give direction to the evaluative process is the development of a master plan as suggested by Zeran and Riccio.[2] The development of such a plan requires that the guidance staff look carefully at the guidance program in terms of its objectives and related activities. By developing and using a master plan, the staff is in a much better position to view each individual activity in relation to the total program.

GATHERING DATA FOR EVALUATION

The selection of procedures to be employed in collecting data for the evaluation process always proceeds from a determination of specific kinds of information that will be needed. Since the desired outcomes of a comprehensive guidance program are numerous and varied, guidance personnel must have familiarity

---

[2] Franklin R. Zeran and Anthony C. Riccio, *Organization and Administration of Guidance Services* (Chicago: Rand McNally and Co., 1963), p. 149.

with a range of procedures if they are to collect the data that will be needed in the evaluation process. The following procedures are suggested as examples of activities which may be effectively employed by guidance workers in scrutinizing their programs.

The Self-Study

Perhaps one of the more logical ways to begin an initial evaluation is the completion of a self-study. Through this procedure, the guidance staff is able to take a comprehensive look at their program and what it is accomplishing. To insure objectivity in the process, it is usually desirable to obtain some type of evaluation guide which will provide a framework of external criteria. Guides of this type are available from a number of sources including the U.S. Office of Education, most state departments of education, the American Personnel and Guidance Association, commercial publishers, and regional accreditation associations.

Most evaluation guides are published in the form of checklists which may be easily used by the guidance staff. Since these guides are usually developed from statements of standards prepared by groups such as regional accreditation associations or professional guidance organizations, they tend to be comprehensive and quite valid in the sense that they represent some degree of consensus among individuals in the guidance profession. For your convenience and understanding, one of the better checklists designed to serve as a guideline to evaluation of guidance services is included here. (See facing page and those following.)

The Case Study

It is often desirable to go beyond the kind of analysis afforded by the self-study and to take an in-depth look at the guidance program within a developmental context, i.e., a context which places the consideration of current trends and developments within the perspective of preceding events and conditions which have influenced the program in its evolvement. Through the utilization of this procedure, consideration is given both to

CHECKLIST FOR APPRAISING THE PROGRAM OF GUIDANCE SERVICES [3]

ASPECTS OF THE PROGRAM	YES	NO

Organizing and Administering the Program of Guidance Services

1. Do the principal and superintendent believe that the guidance program is an important phase of the curriculum and give it consistent administrative support?
2. Have guidance services been identified and accepted by the entire administrative, supervisory, and teaching staff?
3. Is one person responsible for coordination of guidance services?
4. Does the administration utilize the resources of the faculty by delegating appropriate duties in the guidance program to various members?
5. Do teachers, counselors, directors of pupil personnel, school attendance workers, supervisors or instructors, and the entire staff cooperate systematically to meet the needs of individual children?
6. Is there a functioning guidance committee having responsibility for evaluating and recommending changes in the guidance program?
7. Are adequate files and record space provided for the guidance program?
8. Is there a definite well-planned in-service program in operation for improvement of the entire staff in the area of guidance?
9. Are adequate funds allotted in the budget to provide for needed minimal guidance services?
10. Have arrangements been made for resources to help children with unusual problems?

---

[3] Kentucky Department of Education, *Educational Bulletin*, Vol. XXVI, No. 9 (September, 1958), pp. 923–27.

CHECKLIST FOR APPRAISING THE PROGRAM OF GUIDANCE SERVICES (Cont'd.)

ASPECTS OF THE PROGRAM	YES	NO

Individual Inventory Service
1. Is comprehensive information obtained for each pupil in school and brought together in a cumulative record? ___ ___
2. Is the cumulative record passed on as the pupil progresses from grade to grade and from school to school? ___ ___
3. Are provisions made for obtaining information for the cumulative record through:
   a. appropriate tests? ___ ___
   b. visits to homes? ___ ___
   c. case studies? ___ ___
   d. teacher's record of observations of behavior? ___ ___
   e. medical examination results? ___ ___
   f. record of pupil-teacher conference? ___ ___
   g. record of counselor interviews with pupils? ___ ___
4. Are cumulative records easily accessible to all who have valid reason to use them, but only to such persons? ___ ___
5. Are cumulative record data used extensively by teachers to get a complete picture of each pupil? ___ ___
6. Does the testing program include the following types of tests given at regularly scheduled intervals or as needed:
   a. scholastic aptitude (mental ability) tests? ___ ___
   b. standardized achievement tests? ___ ___
   c. interest inventories (in high school only)? ___ ___
   d. special aptitude tests? ___ ___
   e. personality inventories? ___ ___

Information Service
1. Is an adequate information reference section or file maintained as a part of the school library? ___ ___

2. Have community occupational needs and opportunities been determined and kept current? . . ___ ___
3. Are current catalogs of schools and colleges available to high school students? . . . . . ___ ___
4. Is a planned procedure followed to keep students informed about the sources of scholarships and aids? . . . . ___ ___
5. Is there a planned program for helping incoming students become adjusted to the school environment? . . . . ___ ___
6. Is there printed or mimeographed information about the school program and activities? . . ___ ___
7. Is occupational and educational information consistently made available through:
   a. homeroom programs? . . . . . ___ ___
   b. special assembly programs—films, speakers, panels, etc.? . . . . ___ ___
   c. special emphasis in appropriate classroom subjects? . . . . ___ ___

Counseling Service
1. Are the persons doing counseling qualified by training? . . . . ___ ___
2. Have persons designated to do counseling been allotted adequate time in which to do counseling? . ___ ___
3. Do teachers and counselors work cooperatively in helping pupils with their problems? . . . ___ ___
4. Do staff members regard counseling as a professional activity requiring specialized knowledge and skills? . . . . ___ ___
5. Is provision made for referral of children with unusual problems (whether physical, mental, social or emotional) to specialists or community agencies? . . . . ___ ___
6. Is there reasonable assurance that all students needing counseling have opportunity for it? . ___ ___

CHECKLIST FOR APPRAISING THE PROGRAM OF GUIDANCE SERVICES (Cont'd.)

ASPECTS OF THE PROGRAM	YES	NO

Counseling Service (Cont'd.)

7. Do all students have at least one counseling conference a year with a person designated to do counseling? . . . . ___ ___
8. Are all counseling interviews private? . . . ___ ___
9. Are adequate records made of counseling conferences with students? . . . . ___ ___
10. Are pupils assisted in making wise choices about education, vocation, and personal living in terms of each pupil's aptitudes, interests, abilities, and opportunities available? . . . . . . ___ ___
11. Are all school leavers interviewed before leaving school? . . . . ___ ___

Placement Service

1. Are pupils who withdraw or graduate, and want employment helped to secure suitable employment? . . . . ___ ___
2. Is assistance rendered students who need part-time or vacation employment? . . . . . . ___ ___
3. Is a reasonable effort exerted to help each student to:
   a. enter the next step in his education program, or . . . . ___ ___
   b. enter the next step toward reaching his occupational goal, or . . . . ___ ___
   c. take part in appropriate co-curricular activities? . . . . ___ ___

Follow-up Service

1. Are systematic contacts made with former students? . . . . ___ ___
2. Is follow-up information used to improve present educational services in the school? . . . . ___ ___

current status and to past developmental history. Since the case study method goes into considerable depth with its analysis, many of the other procedures discussed in this section may be integrated into the overall project.

Although it is an approach which demands total involvement by members of the guidance staff, the case study approach does provide two types of information that are not generally supplied by other evaluative procedures. First, it provides a basis for deriving a developmental index for the program. Second, it provides an indication concerning the limitations that the community will impose on the further development of the program.[4]

The Survey

One of the more widely used procedures in evaluation is the survey. In general, the survey method is based on assumptions that certain pre-conditions are valid indications of an effective guidance program. Thus, the procedure is designed to determine only the extent to which these pre-conditions are present and cannot be used to validate the underlying assumptions. For example, the guidance staff may feel that the use of the occupational information file contributes to better vocational choices. The survey cannot test this assumption made by the staff, but rather determines the extent to which occupational information files were used.

The survey, as an evaluation procedure, is extremely flexible, and may take a number of forms. The particular type of survey used will, of course, depend on the kind of information needed, the types of respondents, and the ability and resourcefulness of the staff in carrying out the procedure.

In most school situations, it is usually possible to survey the total school population or any part of that population. Where it is not possible to include all individuals within a given population, it is extremely important that appropriate sampling procedures be used to insure that the sample used in the survey is representative of the total population.

---

[4] Zeran and Riccio, *Organization and Administration of Guidance Services*, p. 169.

Regardless of the particular procedure used in the survey, it is also important that the participants be given an appropriate orientation to the project. As one example of what might be done, they may be approached through a letter of explanation designed to elicit total cooperation while, at the same time, avoiding comments which might bias responses. Normally, it will suffice to (a) explain the purposes of the survey, (b) define the participant's role in the project, (c) outline the conditions under which his responses will be received, and (d) make an appeal for the participant's cooperation.

The Questionnaire—The questionnaire is probably the most popular tool in survey research. In content, it varies from items which call for open-ended, free responses to more highly structured items which call for forced choices. Not to be overlooked are the various kinds of personality and adjustment inventories which are produced commercially.

Some of the typical uses of the questionnaire in guidance research are to obtain specific descriptive information about students, to evaluate the extent of use and adequacy of existing services, and to appraise the attitudes and opinions of clients, parents and teachers toward aspects of the guidance program. Counselors attempting to develop questionnaires, especially those assessing attitudes and opinions of various clientele toward their program, will probably find the publication, *Research Guidelines for High School Counselors,* to be helpful.[5]

The first step in developing the questionnaire involves the determination of item universes that are to be included in the instrument, i.e., those attitudes or opinions that are pertinent to the objectives of the study. Once this determination has been made, it is then necessary to develop items which will obtain information needed to answer questions that may be posed with respect to the criteria. If an evaluation master plan has been developed as previously suggested, the criteria that are pertinent

---

[5] Experimental Designs Committee, Assn. for Counselor Education and Supervision, *Research Guidelines for High School Counselors* (New York: College Entrance Examination Board, 1967).

to the survey will already have been identified and are ready to be utilized.

In selecting the form of items in the questionnaire, it is important to keep in mind the specific purposes of the survey and the type of analysis to be conducted at its conclusion. For example, if the researcher is attempting to establish a basis for the development of a frame of reference, the open-ended type of item may be desirable because it is not restrictive to persons who are responding. From the collection of responses, the investigator must then go through a deductive process of cataloging responses until specific patterns are identified. If, on the other hand, the questionnaire is developed within a pre-existing frame of reference, the open-ended item may not be so desirable as the type of item accompanied by specific response categories, i.e., the type of item which is simple to tabulate during the analysis.

If results are to be meaningful, the development and selection of items to be included in a questionnaire should never be done in a haphazard fashion. Once the areas to be included are broken down into the item universes, it is usually wise to ask qualified persons to serve as "judges" in an effort to determine the face validity of the questionnaire, i.e., the extent to which the instrument appears to be gathering the information that it is intended to gather.

Further, the questionnaire should then be field tested with a sample of respondents who are much like the population to be studied. In the field test, particular attention should be given to items which seem to create confusion and which do not produce identifiable response patterns. This feedback should be used to refine the format and utility of the instrument prior to its use in the survey.

If it seems desirable to organize the questionnaire into subsections, the responses obtained during the field test may be used as a basis for determining which categories lend themselves best to such subclassifications. As an alternative, most questionnaire items seem to fall into response categories which may be logically arranged along some type of continuum such as one which extends from most appropriate to least appropriate. Thus, as shown in the example below, it is possible to derive a summated rating scale by assigning quantitative dimensions to each of the categories in terms of relative strength.

On the lines to the right of the items and directly under the numbers 1, 2, 3, 4, or 5, place a check (√) to indicate:

1) I believe this service was MOST APPROPRIATE to me.
2) I believe this service was APPROPRIATE to me.
3) I believe this service was AVERAGE to me.
4) I believe this service was INAPPROPRIATE to me.
5) I believe this service was LEAST APPROPRIATE to me.

Item	Rating
	1 2 3 4 5
Individual counseling received for career planning was . . .	___ ___ ___ ___ ___

This innovation allows greater flexibility in statistical treatment and provides the respondent with a second dimension of response potential, i.e., the degree to which he feels that a particular service is appropriate or inappropriate as opposed to a simple dichotomy. By summing the item ratings, it is then possible to have collective rating scores for each major area and for the questionnaire as a whole. Such scores may then be used for comparison between one school in the system and the next or between one rating period and the next in a particular school. However, until item analysis and reliability checks have been conducted, caution should probably be used in making extensive generalizations from the results.

In most situations, a single type of questionnaire item will not adequately cover the range of information needed to answer questions posed in the research. Therefore, it is usually necessary to incorporate several types of items, each of which is designed to obtain particular kinds of information. A good illustration of a questionnaire containing differential items is herein included for your convenience. Examples of others can be found in Wise, Nordberg, and Reitz.[6]

The following questionnaire is an example of a pupil evaluation questionnaire in counseling: [7]

WHAT I THINK ABOUT COUNSELING IN ⎯⎯⎯⎯⎯⎯⎯
HIGH SCHOOL

1. Do you know your counselor? Yes ⎯⎯ No ⎯⎯
2. Approximately how many times do you see your counselor in a school year? Once ⎯⎯ Twice ⎯⎯ Four times ⎯⎯ Five times ⎯⎯ More ⎯⎯
3. Would you like to talk with your counselor more often? Yes ⎯⎯ No ⎯⎯
4. If you do not see your counselor as often as you would like, why not? ⎯⎯⎯⎯⎯⎯⎯⎯⎯⎯⎯⎯⎯⎯
5. Do you feel free to discuss all of your problems with your counselor? Yes ⎯⎯ No ⎯⎯
6. If you do not discuss your problems with your counselor, with whom do you discuss them? ⎯⎯⎯⎯⎯
7. Have you ever asked the principal to assign you a different counselor? Yes ⎯⎯ No ⎯⎯
8. Mention any problems you can remember having discussed with your counselor.
   a. Educational Problems ⎯⎯⎯⎯⎯⎯⎯⎯⎯⎯

   b. Vocational Problems ⎯⎯⎯⎯⎯⎯⎯⎯⎯⎯

   c. Personal Problems ⎯⎯⎯⎯⎯⎯⎯⎯⎯⎯⎯

   d. Other Problems ⎯⎯⎯⎯⎯⎯⎯⎯⎯⎯⎯⎯
9. Do you feel that your counselor is interested in your problems? Yes ⎯⎯ No ⎯⎯

---

[6] John E. Wise, Robert B. Nordberg, and Donald J. Reitz, *Methods of Research in Education* (Boston: D.C. Heath and Company, 1967), pp. 95–99.

[7] Glenn E. Smith, *Counseling in the Secondary School* (New York: The Macmillan Co., 1955), pp. 299–300.

10. Do you think your counselor has helped you to understand better your aptitudes, interests, abilities, and personality strengths and weaknesses? Yes ___ No ___
11. To what extent would you consider it a personal loss if your high school were to do away with counseling? Great loss ___ Some loss ___ Little loss ___ No loss ___
12. Do you have any suggestions which you think might make counseling more valuable to you? _____

The Interview—A second major tool of survey research is the interview. While it is perhaps most often associated with opinion polls, it has considerable potential for other types of evaluative research in which counselors might engage, especially since counselors would normally have some amount of expertise in interviewing. In some cases, the interview actually becomes an extension of the questionnaire since interviewers frequently use a structured interview as a guide to eliciting specific types of information.

The interview offers distinct advantages in cases where the guidance staff wants to find out why respondents make particular kinds of responses. If the interviewer is skilled, it is possible to focus on key responses and to get beneath the surface to deeper, more significant feelings than those normally reported in a questionnaire. As a survey procedure, the interview is extremely flexible and may be readily adapted to a variety of research needs.

Illustrating how the interview can be effectively used in guidance research, Gutsch and Brumfield surveyed school dropouts in an attempt to identify crucial factors surrounding their withdrawal from school. By using the depth interview as a follow-up to earlier responses recorded on questionnaires, it was possible to understand more completely why respondents answered as they did. It was also possible to understand more profoundly why dropouts actually left school.[8]

---

[8] Kenneth U. Gutsch and Stanley Brumfield, "Depth Interviews: An Innovation in Studying School Dropouts," *Southern Journal of Educational Research,* Vol. II, No. 4 (October, 1968), pp. 265–72.

Perhaps it should be pointed out that the advantage of flexibility within the interview may also become a disadvantage, especially when used by an unskilled person. For those who are interested in interviewing, remember that it is important to receive some training before attempting such a responsibility. If interviewers allow their own personal feelings to influence them, the results will reflect such biases.

In addition it might also be mentioned that the interview is very time-consuming. This factor might be offset through the use of sampling procedures which require that only a small percentage of the total population be surveyed in order to obtain meaningful results.

The Experimental Project

One of the more crucial problems plaguing guidance workers today is the need for validation of assumptions underlying methods and techniques employed in their day-to-day work with students, i.e., the extent to which particular guidance experiences really do seem to make a difference in the subsequent growth and development of students. Counselors, for example, may find it helpful to know what effect, if any, group guidance experiences have had on the ability of students to plan their careers. Because of the difficulty in determining outcomes of activities such as this, counselors are often hard put to defend the use of such procedures. Beyond the guidance staff's own need for confirmation of the procedures they use, it is also becoming increasingly necessary that they be able to validate what they do in order to receive continued support from administrators, teachers, and parents.

One approach for validating guidance procedures, especially those that are new or questionable in terms of value, is to subject the condition in question to experimental study. In essence, the experimental method requires that the effect of other conditions be controlled or held constant in order that the effect of the experimental condition, i.e., the guidance procedure being studied, may become visible and measurable.

While, to be sure, good experimental studies can become quite complex, it is possible for counselors or teachers to engage in functional studies of an experimental nature if proper care and planning is exercised. While it is not the purpose of this book to provide an extensive treatment of experimental design, such resources are readily available. Wise, Nordberg, and Reitz have provided brief guidelines which may assist guidance workers in planning and carrying out experimental studies.[9] In general, experimenters would be well advised to use designs which are appropriate to their level of understanding.

Analysis of Office Records

One of the more useful procedures in obtaining evaluative data is the maintenance and summarization of office records on student use and traffic. In this way the process of evaluation is integrated into the office routine, thus providing a valuable source of cumulative information while at the same time requiring very little extra time for school personnel.

Usually, some type of very brief office form will be filled out for or by each student who uses the guidance services. It need not be involved but simply have places to record the student's name, the data, the reason for seeking services, the services rendered, and the name of the counselor providing services. As an additional procedure, students may be asked to evaluate briefly the assistance given on some type of rating scale or opinionnaire at the culmination of services.

THE FOLLOW-UP SERVICE

The follow-up study deserves special consideration even though it essentially involves the application of the survey procedures just discussed. If properly conducted on a regular basis, the follow-up study, in effect, becomes a part of a major guidance service, i.e., the follow-up service, since it provides the counsel-

---

[9] Wise, Nordberg, and Reitz, *Methods of Research in Education*, pp. 129–44.

ing staff and the school-at-large with continuous feedback from graduates, dropouts, and other former students.

Recognition of the special importance of the follow-up service is based largely on the fact that it is a key source of longitudinal information, and it tends to be particularly descriptive of individual schools. At the same time, as pointed out earlier, it makes a major contribution to the placement service through the contacts it affords with former students and employers in the community. Because of the close relationship between placement and the follow-up service, the individual in charge of placement will typically have the added responsibility for directing follow-up studies.

In the sense that the performance of former students provides some of the more tangible evidence of the school's effectiveness, the follow-up study potentially gathers information which may have usefulness for the administration, the faculty, and other staff members. Specifically, follow-up serves the guidance program and the school in the following ways:

1. Information is provided which may be useful in counseling with students presently in school.
2. Modifications in the school program which are needed to meet the needs of dropouts may be more readily determined.
3. Lines of communication are established and maintained with key persons in the community-at-large.
4. Information concerning the adequacy of existing services assists the guidance staff in making changes and revisions in their program.
5. Information is provided which assists the school in more appropriately making curriculum changes and revisions.
6. Information is provided which helps to identify employment trends in the community as well as the kinds of job opportunities that are open to school leavers.
7. Contacts with former students are maintained and thus provide the school with a continuous index of their development.

Initiating the Follow-up Study

Adequate preparation is extremely important to the success of a good follow-up study. Since the results of a follow-up study may be used by any segment of the school, it is usually wise to enlist the assistance of a steering committee, composed of representatives from the administration, the faculty, and the guidance staff. This steering committee should then be involved in planning and implementing the study.

As an initial step, it is a good idea to orient the steering committee to the purposes of the follow-up study, explaining their role in the project. Questions which should be considered by the committee might include the following:

1. What approaches should be used in contacting those to whom the survey is to be directed?
2. What groups should be included in the study?
3. What procedures will be used to collect, process, and distribute the data?
4. What areas of information should be covered in the study?
5. What costs will be involved?
6. In what form should the results be made available to other school personnel in order to insure maximum utilization?

Implementing the Study

The particular methods used to collect the follow-up data will depend on the kinds of information needed and the ability of the committee to carry out the activity. Most often, the questionnaire will be used because it can be easily mailed to respondents. Also, it offers the dual advantages of adaptability while insuring a reasonable amount of uniformity in the processes of collecting, recording and analyzing the data. In some cases, the interview may be conducted either by telephone or in person, thus offering still greater flexibility to the follow-up procedure.

The subjects to be contacted in a follow-up study would perhaps include former students as well as employers and educators who have had an opportunity to observe post-school performance. In order to differentiate among various types of former students, these students might logically be classified and placed in such major areas of differentiation as dropouts, job-seekers, employed, or college bound, and subclassified in combinations of these areas.

The content of the questionnaire or interview procedure used in the follow-up should be selected by the steering committee and should be designed to answer the questions they feel are important to their school. However, it is sometimes helpful, in the initial development of an instrument, to look at forms used by other school systems. Dean Hummel and Samuel Bonham provide an example of a very comprehensive instrument including a plan for tabulating and analyzing results by IBM computer.[10]

In general, follow-up studies should be conducted often enough to reveal significant changes in the experiences of students who leave the school. Most often, a follow-up of former students conducted every five years will indicate important trends. With other groups, such as those students going into positions of employment, it may be helpful for school personnel to have some feedback on their performance at the end of their first year of employment.

PUTTING RESEARCH FINDINGS TO WORK

All too often, research findings are compiled and then filed away with the faculty and administration having little or no opportunity to utilize the information. This condition points up the need for including the last and final stage of evaluation, i.e., the interpretation and application of findings, in the overall planning for such research. Thus, it is in the roles of interpreter and consultant that the guidance counselor may often provide his greatest service to the administration and the faculty.

---

[10] Dean L. Hummel and Samuel J. Bonham, Jr., *Pupil Personnel Services in Schools* (Chicago: Rand McNally and Co., 1968), pp. 281–91.

Of key importance in putting research findings to work is the extent to which results are shown to have some bearing on specific aspects of the school's program. For example, research will have significance for a particular teacher when he realizes that the findings may help him do a more effective job in his area.

As an initial step in preparing the findings of a study for presentation to school personnel, the analyses should be summarized and, as nearly as possible, be related to various educational processes in operational terms. It is usually helpful, in summarizing findings, to depict trends and relationships on some medium such as a profile sheet or a graph. If comparisons are made between various departments within the school or with other school systems, care should be taken not to threaten school personnel whose departments may be affected. In general, such comparisons should be made in a manner which will point toward positive steps for improvement rather than simply identify weaknesses or shortcomings.

Once the preliminary work of analyzing and summarizing the research findings has been completed, it is then possible to meet with the other school personnel to go over the materials in detail. While this type of information can sometimes be shared in large groups, it is perhaps most effectively done with small groups selected on a basis of their particular areas of work. It is usually a good idea to prepare copies of the research summaries for distribution to the participants, allowing them to use the information for future reference.

In summary, the research process, as it relates to the evaluation of educational outcomes, is not complete until the results have been shared with all interested parties in a form which they can understand and use. If such an approach is incorporated, evaluation becomes highly functional to the school and makes possible the support necessary for a wider range of research activities. Collectively, these studies may provide the guidance staff and the school-at-large with sounder bases for approaching critical educational decisions.

9

IDEAS FOR ORGANIZING AND ADMINISTERING THE GUIDANCE PROGRAM

Many of our present day authors have concerned themselves more with the theoretical aspect of organizing a guidance program than with the functional aspect. Since each guidance program has many unique counterparts, it would seem that initiating each new program would serve as a source of many new experiences as well as a reflection of numerous past experiences. As we have already said, guidance, if it is to be carried out systematically, must have both leadership and cooperation. Perhaps H. J. Otto closely approached an identical conceptualization when he said:

> Every worthy undertaking, if it is to be carried forward effectively, requires a scheme of operations. Usually one of the first things a leader does is to develop a plan whereby steps may be taken toward an objective. If the leadership operates in terms of democratic principles, such plans are developed in cooperation with other persons involved. The result is an organization during which and within which persons operate in discharging their various responsibilities and contributions to the enterprise.[1]

---

[1] Henry J. Otto, *Elementary School Organization and Administration* (New York: Appleton-Century-Crofts Company, Educational Division, Meredith Corporation, 1950), p. 237.

STRUCTURING THE PROGRAM

Where Are We Now?—Assuming that the person responsible for initiating the guidance program has a working knowledge of guidance as well as the necessary facilities, then it seems apparent that the organization of guidance services requires two main ingredients, i.e., (a) leadership and (b) cooperation. Without these, guidance, like many other aspects of education, cannot function effectively. It is probably safe to say that the success or failure in organizing guidance activities will, to a large extent, depend upon the acceptance of guidance by the school administrator, his staff, and the entire faculty. Such cooperation has a strong tendency to prevent the overlapping of activities, the duplication of efforts, and the general confusion found among faculty members. It might also be mentioned at this point that before any attempt is made to organize a program of guidance, or for that matter any school program, participants of the program should be permitted a period of time during which they may consider the basic principles relative to the program. Roeber, Smith and Erickson make the following helpful suggestions for introducing any program:

1. Any service, whether new or old, needs the acceptance and leadership of the school administrator.
2. The success of a program depends upon a state of readiness of the school staff to accept, contribute to, and utilize the service.
3. The objectives of any service have to be clearly defined.
4. The development of a service has to evolve from existing services and be adapted to the unique circumstances inherent in any school setting.
5. A service has to be developed in harmony with the total educational program of the school.[2]

---

[2] Edward C. Roeber, Glenn E. Smith, and Clifford E. Erickson, *Organization and Administration of Guidance Services* (New York: McGraw-Hill Book Company, 1955), pp. 26–27.

Where Are We Going?—Concerned as we are with a practical or functional approach to guidance, it appears that the question most frequently asked is, "How can a school organize a program of services?" To assist in answering such a question, the authors have listed nine basic steps which they recommend for the organization of guidance services:

1. Survey both the faculty and the student body in an attempt to determine what services are needed.
2. Confer with teachers and administrators to determine what facilities and resources are available for financing projects which may extend themselves beyond the recommended budget.
3. Define and clarify the objectives of the guidance services program taking into account such things as the student needs from which these services arise and the philosophy of the school program for which they are designed.
4. Assign specific responsibilities to faculty members who are willing to assist in the development of better guidance services.
5. Allocate responsibility to faculty members on the basis of their respective abilities and relative to their desire to become involved.
6. Delegate to each faculty or staff member assigned a guidance responsibility, authority commensurate with that responsibility.
7. Define and clarify the working relationships among individuals so that those who are carrying out specific guidance responsibilities understand how best to utilize those guidance responsibilities that are being carried out by other individuals.
8. Keep the focus of attention on the student and his needs.
9. Keep the method of operation as simple as possible.

Preliminary to this consideration, however, it appears that the essential steps which must be weighed most heavily in planning a guidance program are as follows:

1. To have the chief administrator of the institution assume the responsibility and initiative for instituting the program.
2. To hold faculty meetings for the purpose of developing a philosophy of guidance.
3. To analyze the present program in terms of three basic questions: (a) What has been done to develop a guidance program? (b) What objectives have been set for the further development of such a program? (c) What is the best possible way to make the transition from (a) to (b)?
4. To appoint a Guidance Committee or an advisory council to serve the needs of the school system effectively.
5. To appoint a chairman of the Guidance Committee or advisory council.
6. To plan both long-range and short-range objectives.
7. To adopt a testing program which will meet the needs of the institution.
8. To provide an in-service training program which will assist teachers in understanding guidance techniques.
9. To make provisions for collecting and recording data about pupils.
10. To make provisions for collecting occupational and educational information.
11. To make provisions for filing occupational and educational information.
12. To define guidance and guidance purposes to the community.
13. To select as counselors people who have the interest, ability and qualities necessary for counseling.
14. To secure the cooperation of local clubs and community organizations in helping to set realistic objectives for students while at the same time making guidance effective in the school setting.

How Will We Get There?—Up to now some attempt has been made to emphasize the importance of careful planning and proper orientation in putting a program of guidance into operation.

It is only natural for one to believe that effective guidance is brought about through a logical pattern of organization, but, of course, there will be some concern as to how we arrive at this plan. Since each school setting is unique in itself, it would appear that no organizational plan developed for use in any given school can be superimposed upon a second school. In essence, it seems reasonable to believe that if a program of guidance is to be successful, it should be organized in terms of presently existing services and personnel who are best able to perform these services. Possibly Roeber, Smith, and Erickson have captured the feeling of a flexible approach in pointing out that two types of organizational patterns emerge as basic to all others. Type I is a program in which the administrator is responsible for policy making, and Type II is a program in which a committee of faculty members is responsible for setting the policy. Examples of these two patterns are shown below.[3]

Plan for Type I

```
                    Superintendent
                          |
                     Principal --------- Advisory
        Teachers -----    |              Guidance Committee
                     Counselor  -------  (Optional)
                          |
                       Pupils
```

——— Administrative Relationship
- - - - Cooperative Relationship

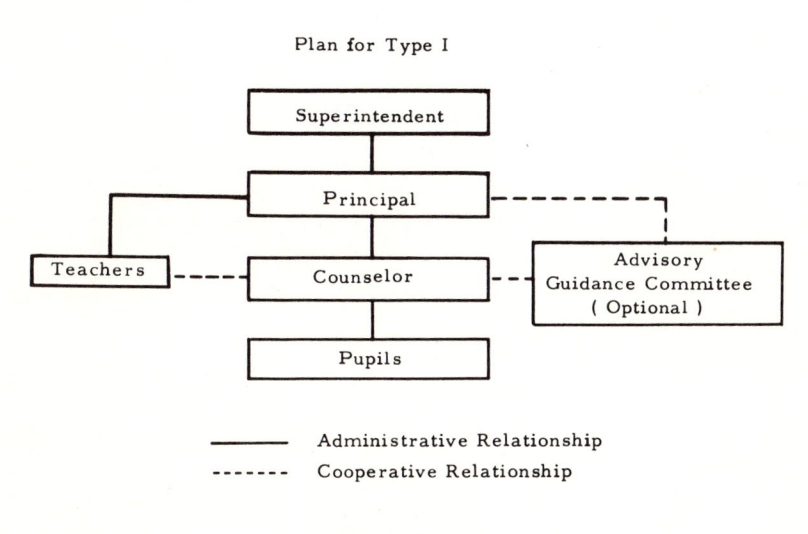

Figure 9–1.

[3] Roeber, Smith, and Erickson, *Organization and Administration of Guidance Services,* p. 33.

The Type I method of plotting relationships for the guidance services implies several conclusions and suggestions which affect its successful operation.[4]

First, the administration officer of the school, the principal, assumes direct responsibility for establishing guidance policies.

Second, the counselor's position may vary along a continuum from an administrative relationship to a cooperative relationship with respect to staff members.

Third, the responsibility for carrying out guidance policies is centered in one individual, who because of his training, is capable of implementing those policies.

Fourth, although it is optional, utilization of an advisory Guidance Committee of administrators and staff members may often be of value in connection with the Type I Plan of Organization.[5]

Plan for Type II

```
                    ┌──────────────────┐
                    │  Superintendent  │
                    └────────┬─────────┘
                             │
                    ┌────────┴─────────┐
          ┌─────────│    Principal     │─────────┐
          │         └────────┬─────────┘         │
          │                  │                   │
    ┌─────┴────┐   ┌─────────┴─────────┐   ┌─────┴─────┐
    │ Teachers │---│ Guidance Committee│---│ Counselor │
    └─────┬────┘   └─────────┬─────────┘   └─────┬─────┘
          │                  ┊                   │
          │         ┌────────┴─────────┐         │
          └─────────│      Pupils      │─────────┘
                    └──────────────────┘
```

------ Cooperative Relationship
———— Administrative Relationship

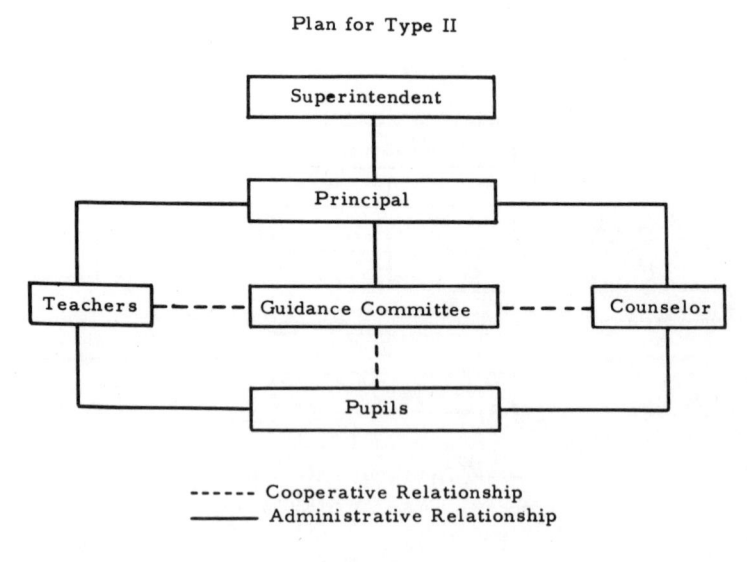

Figure 9–2.

---

[4] *Ibid.*, p. 33.
[5] *Ibid.*, pp. 33–34.

The Type II organizational pattern focuses attention upon the Guidance Committee which may be used at both elementary and secondary school levels.[6]

What are the functions of this committee?

1. It studies the needs, purposes, and procedures essential to the development of guidance services and sets necessary guidance policies.
2. It keeps administrators and staff members informed of its activities and policy decisions, frequently drawing out their reactions to policies and practices.
3. It coordinates and evaluates all guidance activities and services in the school.
4. It plans any in-service professional development activities in guidance services for staff members and administrators.[7]

In order to function properly, the Type II pattern requires the presence of the following conditions in the school setting:

First, the principal delegates guidance policy making to a committee and actively supports the resulting policies.

Second, the fact that the Guidance Committee is responsible for cooperative policy making permits the counselor to remain a staff member.

Third, the implementation of guidance policies is in the hands of one individual, the counselor.

Fourth, the Guidance Committee is composed of those individuals who are interested in guidance services and represent different academic interests and all educational levels.[8]

GETTING STAFF MEMBERS INVOLVED

In order to make the plan of organization effective, it becomes increasingly apparent that a strong in-service training program is

---

[6] *Ibid.*, p. 36.
[7] *Ibid.*, pp. 35–36.
[8] *Ibid.*, pp. 36–38.

necessary. Once the faculty members understand what guidance is, it is simply a matter of finding out how well they fit into the organizational pattern and where they can best serve. Some principles suggested for carrying out an in-service training program in guidance are:

1. Always attempt to start with faculty background. A great deal of guidance is done by faculty members who have some background in guidance and have attempted to carry this experience to the pupils. Such instructors should be given credit for what has been done.

2. Try to build the guidance program on a foundation of faculty interest. The program should arise from problems which are common to faculty members.

3. Carry out the in-service training during school hours.

4. Make every effort to plan with the faculty.

5. Have the principal participate in the program whenever possible and thus reflect an active interest in the program. It will be found that the role of the administrator is always of primary importance in the success of a guidance program and for this reason should be carefully studied.

The Administrator's Responsibility

The school administrator is the responsible head of the school system. As such, he will provide administrative leadership for the guidance program. Responsibilities relative to this position frequently require that the administrator—

1. Create among staff members and community an awareness of the need for guidance services.
2. Budget a sufficient amount of funds to support adequately the program.
3. Delegate to a qualified person or persons the responsibility for providing leadership, supervision, and direction in developing and coordinating the service.
4. Provide for physical facilities, materials and clerical services essential to an effective guidance program.
5. Provide adequate time, staff and aid in arranging a

satisfactory schedule for carrying out the services of the guidance program.[9]

The Teacher's Responsibility

If guidance is to be continuous in the school, it is desirable that the teachers possess an understanding of the nature of guidance as it relates to their work.

In 1945 a conference of state supervisors concluded that guidance in the public school is a joint function of the entire faculty, i.e., superintendent, principal, classroom and homeroom teachers, and those engaged in specialized services, as well as the counselor. If the guidance program is recognized as a joint function, then it follows that each person involved in this function has some responsibility in connection with it. The major guidance responsibilities set forth by the conference committee relative to the classroom teacher are as follows:

In the area of the individual inventory:

1. Assist in the compilation of the cumulative record.
2. Keep pupil's individual inventory up to date.
3. Have a thorough knowledge of every pupil in his group.
4. Furnish the counselor information to aid in parent contacts.

In the phase of occupational information:

1. Cooperate with school counselors in dissemination of occupational information.
2. Contribute occupational information from his own specialized field.
3. Stress, with careful regard to realistic conditions, the occupational value of subjects taught.
4. Provide developmental group activities in citizenship, leadership, and personality.
5. Explain the importance of traits of character and personality needed to become a successful worker.

---

[9] Kentucky State Department of Education, *Educational Bulletin: Guidance Services*, Vol. XXXIV, No. 9 (September, 1966), pp. 20–21.

6. Help the student to evaluate important outcomes of successful work in addition to salary.
7. Encourage the student to work up to capacity.
8. Assist in preparing assembly program dealing with vocational guidance.
9. Interpret the vocational implications of school subjects and help students to develop proper work attitudes.
10. Assist the counselor in arranging and carrying out occupational trips.
11. Assist in the development of poster materials, plays, and similar activities related to guidance.
12. Encourage the use of visual and auditory aids.

In the field of counseling:

1. Be on the alert for interests, aptitudes, plans, and behavior patterns which the student's counselor should know about.
2. Direct to the counselor those individuals who need specialized help.
3. Serve on committees related to the guidance program.
4. Study and practice good interviewing and counseling procedures to make any counseling that he may be asked to do more effective.[10]

The Counselor's Responsibilities

The duties of the counselor are, of course, unique to his background and training. Some of the responsibilities generally assumed by people in this field are:

1. Coordinating the guidance program within the school under the direction of the principal and faculty guidance committee, and performing a liaison function between the school and community counseling resources and facilitating their use by teachers and pupils.
2. Counseling with pupils on matters of self-understanding, long-range educational and vocational plans, secondary school program planning, academic

---

[10] Clifford P. Froehlich, *Guidance Services in Smaller Schools* (New York: McGraw-Hill Book Company, 1950), pp. 59–61.

achievement, post-high school educational and vocational opportunities and placement, social and personal development. This is the counselor's major responsibility.
3. Providing for and participating in group guidance programs with emphasis on orientation, effective study methods, educational and vocational planning, personal and social development, and group leadership.
4. Assisting teachers in developing guidance units, obtaining and interpreting information about pupils, appropriate use of cumulative records, providing guidance aids, materials and services for pupils.
5. Assisting in providing and interpreting to parents, information on individual pupil's strengths and limitations and problems of young people. Encouraging, when necessary, parental participation in case conferences related to pupil growth and development.
6. Supervising the formulation and maintenance of a cumulative record system.
7. Participating in developing a group standardized testing program.
8. Supervising the administration of standardized group tests.
9. Sharing in the development and maintenance of informational resources related to summer school, job and vocational explorations, summer and part-time employment, post-high school educational opportunities and post-high school employment.
10. Knowing the community, its resources, placement opportunities, and expectations.[11]

TYPICAL PROBLEMS IN ORGANIZING A GUIDANCE PROGRAM

There are many obstacles to organizing a program of guidance services just as there are problems to organizing any program.

---
[11] Kentucky State Department of Education, *Educational Bulletin: Guidance Services,* Vol. XXXIV, No. 9 (September, 1966), p. 21.

Many of these obstacles result from mistakes which could have been avoided at the time the program was introduced. Some of the mistakes which frequently occur in the systematic development of a program of guidance services are:

1. The inability to clarify and define the objectives of the program in terms of the objectives of the total school program.
2. The inability to develop proper staff relations and well-defined patterns of responsibility among staff members.
3. The inability to work out a method of operation without duplicating the services and responsibilities that have already been carried out or assigned.
4. The inability to establish and maintain harmony among staff members.
5. The inability to gain support for the program or to maintain and increase such support once it has been gained.

If precautions are carefully taken to avoid these mistakes, guidance services will meet with fewer obstacles and less outright opposition. With these principles of organization well in mind, there remains still another factor for consideration in the organization of a guidance program. This consideration must be focused on the coordination of guidance services at the district level. At the district level it appears that the term "pupil personnel services" will become increasingly important and that the person responsible for this position will be referred to as a coordinator of pupil personnel services or as a director of pupil personnel services. In most cases he will be directly responsible to the superintendent of schools and will serve as the coordinator of the (1) pupil accounting service, (2) health service, (3) remedial education service, (4) speech/hearing correction service, (5) home/school social service, (6) parent education service, (7) counseling and guidance service, (8) assessment service, and (9) research service. One of the basic ingredients essential to such coordination is the principle of staff communication.

THE PRINCIPLE OF STAFF COMMUNICATION

Perhaps of all the responsibilities the guidance counselor has, his ultimate success will depend on his ability to coordinate and handle problems in such a way as to facilitate solutions in an expeditious manner. The principle of "staff communication" is simply one idea which he can apply to become more efficient and more effective as a guidance counselor.

Completed staff communication involves the study of a problem and the presentation of a solution. It can be done by a counselor, by a guidance committee, or through the utilization of a staff approach whereby teachers and other staff members who are familiar with the problem get together in an effort to resolve the problem. The idea is to reach a consensus which can be spelled out in writing and placed before the head administrator for his consideration. If, as a counselor, your method of operation includes a comprehensive study of each problem before it is written up and communicated to the head administrator, such action makes your chances of an honest evaluation by the administrator much more feasible.

The inexperienced counselor is sometimes impulsive and in his haste to bring a problem or an idea to the attention of the chief administrator he loses some of the detail. Instead of becoming meaningful the situation reduces itself to one of utter frustration. The counselor finds himself unable to communicate his idea because he has not really entertained the idea long enough to understand the many facets it has. As a result the administrator asks questions which cannot be answered at this time and the counselor is unable to define clearly and concisely those aspects of the idea that are essential to the development or progress of the guidance program.

Counselors might find it to their advantage to study an idea and to write and rewrite the idea until it is clearly and concisely expressed. To do so makes it possible for the counselor to place a written concept of what he wants before the administrator and to discuss intelligently those sections of the communiqué which may have to be explained in greater detail. To approach a relationship with an administrator or with a staff member in this way reflects the very best that the counselor has to offer. Whether or not the idea is accepted or rejected is not so important as is the fact that within the confines of his limitations he has presented the idea at its best. Without such a presentation, it would have had no real opportunity for success. As a final check before submitting a written idea to the chief administrator these questions should be asked:

"If I were the head administrator, would I be willing to accept this idea—would I be willing to sign this paper and agree to take the responsibility for the statements I have made?"

If a counselor's answer is yes, he is undoubtedly prepared. If his answer is no, a better presentation may be in order.

GETTING PEOPLE INVOLVED

Several years ago a counselor telephoned my office and said that his school was about to be evaluated by an accrediting association. He was rather apprehensive about the situation because very few of the students knew that the school in which he was working offered guidance services. What the counselor wanted was some direct method of contacting all the students and blessing them with his many academic endowments. Since there is no quick way of communicating guidance services to youngsters and since his past five years as a counselor at this school had obviously been less fruitful than he would have liked, I gave him this answer: "It seems that your only alternative is to hold an assembly program and to tell the students that although you haven't served them for the past five years, you do have an office in the school." Needless to say, the counselor hung up and has never discussed the point further.

Those of you who are in guidance realize that all the ideas entertained throughout this book are, in fact, ideas that help the guidance counselor to function more effectively. Without personal commitment and total personal involvement within the confines of his work, the counselor will seldom, if ever, find the operation of a guidance program successful.

However, in behalf of the counselor's original plea for assistance, we continued to explore methods of taking guidance to parents and community members as well as to faculty members. In addition to the many concepts introduced in this book, it now seems that a counselor might make a rather basic but direct approach to communicating his guidance program by accepting and preparing for speaking engagements. To test the feasibility of such an approach we have collected and tested a number of stories which we now feel lend themselves well to many situations in which a counselor finds himself.

COMMUNICATING IDEAS THROUGH FOLKLORE

The first story is one which, in its own unique way, assists people to understand what we are talking about when we use such terms as integration and involvement. We have used this story many times not only to assist an audience to move from awareness to consciousness—from a point of knowing about something to a point of actually experiencing it—but to understand the purpose of life and to introduce the idea that MAN may actually be the product of his efforts rather than the residue of impersonal forces which push and pull him through life. The story goes like this:

The Fountain

In the long ago days, before men sold dreams for gold and fine raiment to display before their neighbors, there lived Aaron, a man honored and respected by his fellow-villagers as an honest and successful man. He had taken the small patrimony which had descended to him from his father and his father's father, and had cultivated it with care and diligence. He had a loving wife, and had raised his children to adulthood with kindness to be an honor to his village and his family.

But now, as he stood on the summit of his life and looked to the descent which needs must reach unto death, he was distressed and troubled. He cursed the mortality of his ancestors. He became envious of his own sons—envious of their youth and strength and length of days. He was querulous with his patient wife, and compared the dreams of his youth with the present bland reality. His words were given to petty fault-finding—often forgetting a lifetime of kindness and patience for a small but more recent slight. Memories of past disappointments, even of the kindly guidance and childhood discipline of his parents, rankled his soul and disturbed the peace of his slumbers. Often, the rising sun and the morning songs of awakening birds brought to his lips not a paean of praise for another dawn but a curse for the continuation of life's dissatisfactions. Anger clouded his days, and the rage in his heart isolated him from his fellow-man like a hedge of thorns.

One night after hours of fretful tossing on his bed he had a dream. In this dream he saw a beautiful marble fountain carved with great art, showing the procession of life as going to a temple. Then he saw that the fountain was built between two gravestones, and he knew he was at the final resting-place of his parents. There, on the base of the fountain, he saw his gray-haired father sitting in quiet ease. And his father spoke in a gentle voice, as had always been his wont, "Son, come: Sit a while here with me."

As the father moved in his seat to make him room, the dreamer saw on the base of the fountain an inscription: "Drink and refresh yourself. He who drinks will never die."

Aaron looked at his father and asked, "Is this true?"

And the dream-father nodded, and motioned with his hand to the pool at the fountain's base.

As the dreamer hesitated, the shadow reached for a small silver cup, filled it with water from the fountain, and gave it to his son.

As Aaron was about to drink, he saw reflected in the bottom of the cup his long-dead mother's youthful face.

At this recognition, he startled, awakened, and the dream was ended. Aaron found himself sitting, with beating heart, in his own bed, staring at the shadows on the moon-patched wall.

It was a troubled man who walked the village streets the next day, and again the next. He could not share his dream even with his wife, nor could be obliterate the vision.

On the third day Aaron could contain himself no more and found his way to the hillside burial plot where for generations the dead of the village had been laid in quiet slumber. It had been a long time since he had been there to visit the family burial place. At last he found the overgrown graves of his parents. He recognized the gravestones from his dreams, but here in reality there was no marble fountain—only weeds and some old bits of pottery from a now long-broken vase that had once held flowers from the homeside garden. Sadly disillusioned and troubled, he returned to his home.

Now a strange, melancholy, but quiet sadness fell upon Aaron; and the contrast between the fountain by the graves in the dream and the weed-overgrown ancestral graves on the hillside haunted him.

The next day, with his youngest son, he took garden-tools to the burial acre to clear the family plot of weeds. As they worked, Aaron found the companionship of the young, strong son a pleasure long neglected. While resting in the noon-day shade and over their frugal repast of wine and bread, the father recounted his dream. The son, a youth of imaginative and poetic nature, joyed in the unaccustomed confidence of the father. He asked many questions about the fountain and the scenes depicted thereon, until the dream-fountain came to live in his heart with more reality than if it were carved of alabaster and fine gold.

As the sun was beginning to sink and their work was completed, the two stood for a minute admiring the new-cleared headstones. Suddenly the view of the village, as seen between the headstones, took on the form of the carved fountain showing the procession of life, for there, etched clearly against the evening sun, were the villagers returning from their fields. With a startled cry the son pointed to the scene, but both had recognized the picture on the fountain at the same instant.

In a move, half mocking and half frightened, the son turned to the father and cried, "Now, if we could find the real fountain and drink from it, we—you and I—will live forever!"

Matching act to thought, and before the father could stop him, he took his spade; and mid-way between the two gravestones, broke sod.

Ere he could move his spade, there, up from the deep earth, bubbled a small trickle of water.

Excitedly, the young man dropped to his knees and tried to drink from his hands, but the crystal water eluded him and only muddied his fingers. Then, snatching the empty wine bottle left from their mid-day repast, he lowered the bottle into the little grave-like trench and allowed the water to flow gently down the slender neck of the flask. When about one wine-glass-full of water had been gathered, the fountain slowly receded, dwindled, and lost itself in the dark earth—and was gone. Further digging could not recover the precious fountain; only the now damp and pungent earth remained.

In their hurried digging they had forgotten the wine bottle with its precious contents; but when darkness ended their quest and the earth had been smoothed over the phantom fountain, like a new-made grave, there stood the wine-bottle, with its priceless clear water, leaning against the parental headstone as if held in kindly hands.

Quite beside himself now, the son grasped the bottle and cried, "Thank God! Now we will see!" And he raised the bottle to his lips.

Before he could drink, the eyes of the two men met; then the son slowly lowered the bottle and, with a kindly gesture, gave it to his father.

"You, my father, are old. I am young. I have a long time in which to dig for mine own fountain. Drink, and be my father forever."

Gently the father took the proffered bottle from his son's hand. Quietly he wiped off the damp soil with his sleeve. Putting the hand-carved stopper carefully deep into the neck of the bottle he said to his son, "Our precious water is safe. Now we can wait. Tomorrow is another day."

For one brief moment the two watched the village scene with its now-twinkling lights as framed between the two headstones; and then, picking up their tools, they set out for their home below.

"Let us say nothing about our dreams," said the old man.

"Let us keep the bottle safe," said the son.

Days passed. The father envied not the son's youth and strength, for he knew he could drink the one draught rescued from the priceless fountain. And the son envied not the father's wisdom, for they could share it, even as they shared the secret of the dream and the bottle.

Both could now work and share in the vision of the fountain depicting the procession of life between the parental headstones. So busy with human affairs were their days that the secret wine-bottle was all but forgotten in the press of new life ever welling up from the damp earth in due season.

In its proper time the man, full of years and peaceful weariness, quietly withdrew and counted the end of his days.

When recognition of the beginning of the end dawned upon the youngest son, he suddenly remembered the dream-fountain and the wine-bottle with its life-giving water.

Bringing the precious bottle from its dusty hiding place in the wall, he placed it into his dying father's hands and begged, "Drink now, Father. I can not bear to have you leave me and my children."

Aaron took the bottle gently. He remembered the day when the son once before had withheld his own thirst and had given the bottle to him so that he, the father, might have a new lease on life, a life gone dead with unforgiven sins.

"It has been a pleasant journey, my son," the father replied. "It has been a beautiful dream.

"Now leave me for a few minutes," he continued. "Even as you would not drink before me that afternoon, so will I not drink before you now. Come back in a little while."

When the son returned, the bottle was empty, and old Aaron sat quietly in his chair.

"My faith could carry me only this far. I could not drink

it alone, and there was not enough for us all. I watered yon potted flower with the water from our dream-fountain. Carry it with me to the place where we found it."

As they watched, they saw the petals of the flower slowly opening in the spring sunshine.[12]

Turning to the old man now, and looking at him in his final moments of life, the son realized that the essence of life is in the journey and that the old man realized that his purpose was ultimately to return to the light whence he had come. This then was his challenge: to recognize that he himself was the product of his efforts and that the challenges of life were only tests of his ability to transcend his status quo, to persevere as an individual dedicated to the cause of becoming one—to the cause of finding his commonality among men. Both he and his son had learned that life is only one step in a long journey back to the very essence of existence—the very light of life—back to God.

A second story which we frequently use is one which illustrates morality. Although it is rather short, we find it most effective when working with PTA groups—especially when attempting to communicate an understanding of adult responsibility. The story helps to focus the attention of the audience without seeming to reprimand. In effect, it is a nice way of communicating something which, in many instances, must be said.

It's O.K. Son, Everybody Does It

When Johnny was six years old, he was with his father when they were caught speeding. His father handed the officer a five-dollar bill with his driver's license. "It's O.K., Son," his father said as they drove off. "Everybody does it."

When he was eight, he was permitted at a family council, presided over by Uncle George, on the surest means to shave points off the income tax return. "It's O.K., Kid," his uncle said. "Everybody does it."

When he was nine, his mother took him to his first

---

[12] Arthur L. Rautman, "The Fountain," *Voices: The Art and Science of Psychotherapy*, Vol. 3, No. 3 (Fall, 1967), pp. 97–99.

theater production. The box office man couldn't find any seats until his mother discovered an extra two dollars in her purse. "It's O.K., Son," she said. "Everybody does it."

When he was 12, he broke his glasses on the way to school. His Aunt Francine persuaded the insurance company that they had been stolen and they collected $27. "It's O.K., Kid," she said. "Everybody does it."

When he was 15, he made right guard on the high school football team. His coach showed him how to block and at the same time grab the opposing tackle by the shirt so the official couldn't see it. "It's O.K., Kid," the coach said. "Everybody does it."

When he was 16, he took his first summer job at the big market. His assignment was to put the overripe tomatoes in the bottom of the boxes and the good ones on top where they would show. "It's O.K., Kid," the manager said. "Everybody does it."

When he was 18, Johnny and a neighbor applied for a college scholarship. Johnny was a marginal student. His neighbor was in the upper three percent of his class, but he couldn't play right guard. Johnny got the assignment. "It's O.K., Kid," they told him. "Everybody does it."

When he was 19, he was approached by an upper classman who offered the test answers for three dollars. "It's O.K., Kid," he said. "Everybody does it."

Johnny was caught and sent home in disgrace. "How could you do this to your mother and me?" his father said. "You never learned anything like this at home." His aunt and uncle were also shocked.

If there's one thing the adult world can't stand, it's a kid who cheats. . . .[13]

The third story is one which illustrates the practical use of semantics. That is, it assists individuals to understand the need to become more definitive when they express themselves. Since so many counselors, teachers, students, and parents frequently communicate without recognizing the serious implications of

---

[13] Jack Griffin, "It's O.K. Son, Everybody Does It," *Guideposts* (August, 1965), p. 25. Reprinted with permission from the *Chicago Sun-Times*.

what they are saying, this story illustrates extremely well the idea that it makes a great deal of difference just how one asks a question.

Two Priests

A story is told about two priests. They were arguing whether it was proper to smoke and to pray at the same time. One said "Yes," the other "No." To settle the matter they decided that both should write to the Holy Father for his opinion. Sometime later they met and compared notes. Each claimed that the Holy Father had supported his view. They were perplexed. Finally one asked, "How did you phrase your question?" The other replied: "I asked whether it was proper to smoke while one is praying; and the Pope answered, 'Certainly not, praying is serious business and permits no distractions.' And how did you phrase your question?" "Well," said the other, "I asked if it were proper to pray while smoking, and the Pope answered, 'Certainly, prayer is always in order.'" [14]

Although the fourth story we use is rather brief, it has a unique way of bringing people to a more profound level of understanding since it carries with it some feelings about MAN's destiny, his personal commitment to life, and the world of work. Both students and parents have found it meaningful and have become more interested in the guidance services we offer because we have communicated with them in this way. Because of its extreme appropriateness for so many occasions, we now pass it along to you as one final thought to remember when working with young people.

One Solitary Life

Here is a man who was born in an obscure village, the child of a peasant woman. He worked in a carpenter shop until he was 30, and then for three years he was an itinerant preacher. He never held an office. He never owned a home. He never wrote a book. He never had a family.

---

[14] Gordon Allport, "Psychological Models for Guidance," *Harvard Educational Review,* Vol. 32, No. 4 (Fall, 1962), p. 377.

He never went to college. He never put his foot inside a big city. He never traveled 200 miles from the place where he was born. He never did one of the things which usually accompany greatness. He had no credentials but himself.

While he was a young man, the tide of public opinion turned against him. His friends ran away. He was turned over to his enemies. He went through the mockery of a trial. He was nailed to a cross between two thieves. While he was dying, his executioners gambled for the only piece of property he had on earth, and that was his coat. When he was dead, he was laid in a private grave through the pity of a friend.

Nineteen wide centuries have come and gone, and today he is the central figure of the human race and the leader of the column of progress.

I am far within the mark when I say that all the armies that ever marched, and all the navies that were ever built, and all the parliaments that ever sat, and all the kings that ever reigned, put together, have not affected the life of man upon this earth, as that One Solitary Life.[15]

---

[15] James A. Francis, *One Solitary Life*.

INDEX

A

Achievement:
  understanding poor performance, 93–95, 118–125
Allport, Gordon, 237
Anecdotal record, 23
Anxiety, 102
  illustrative case, 102–110
  separation anxiety, 123–124
Assistance to other agencies, 140
Astin, A. W., 150
Autobiography, 21

B

Bennett, Margaret E., 80
Blom, Gaston, 125
Bonham, Samuel J., 184
Bowen, M., 125
Bradley, C., 125
Brumfield, Stanley, 180

C

Calvert, Robert, Jr., 161
Checklist, 22
Circle, D. F., 151
Clemens, D. B., 151
Committee:
  faculty, 24
  guidance, 27, 191–193
Community agencies, 141
  apprenticeship program, 144
  auxiliary capacity, 141
  church sponsored guidance programs, 144
  private employment agencies, 142
  selection of, 144
  state employment services, 143
  state Vocational Rehabilitation Service, 143
  table of services, 146–147
  Veterans Administration Counseling Program, 143
Community survey, 151
  class project, 151
  follow-up study, 153
  occupational, 136, 151
  pre-planning, 152
  using directories, 152
Counseling:
  anxiety, study of, 102, 110

Counseling (*Cont.*)
  basic orientation, 110–111
  counselor's role, 111–112
  definitions, 116
  experiential syndrome, 98–99
  goals and purposes, 98–99
  human encounter, 97–102
  ideas, 99–102
  illustrative case, 102–110
  innovations, 97–102
  placement, 138
  precounseling orientation, 94–97
  relationship to guidance, 110–111
Craig, M., 127
Creativity, 125–126
Cumulative record, 18, 30, 131

D

Data processing, 162
  in placement, 162
Delinquency:
  prediction, 126–127
  screening instruments, 126–127
Depression, 94–95
Diary, 21
Dictionary of Occupational Titles, 69
Dyslexia, 118–123
  detection, 119–120
  emotional effect, 119
  illustrative case, 121–123

E

Elementary schools:
  guidance services, 117
Ellis, A., 105
Environmental assessment, 150
  college environments, 150
  use of data, 150
Erickson, Clifford E., 188, 191

Ethics:
  defined through folklore, 201–208
Evaluation:
  basic tasks, 167
  characteristics of evaluation program, 166–167
  collecting data, 169
  defining objectives, 167
  developing criteria, 168
  master plan, 169
  measurement and assessment, 168-169
  rationale, 165
  specific purposes, 165–166
Evaluative procedures:
  case study, 171, 174
  checklist, 171–174
  experimental project, 181
  follow-up service, 183–184
  interview, 180
  questionnaire, 176
  records used, 182
  self study, 171
  survey, 174
Expectancy Gap: 145, 148–150, 154–155
Experiential syndrome, 96–99, 145
  illustrative stories, 201–208
Experimental method:
  source for further study, 182
  validating guidance procedures, 180

F

Feather, Don B., 41
Follow-Up Service:
  initiation, 184
  serving the guidance program, 183
  use of steering committee, 184
Forrester, G., 154

INDEX

Francis, James A., 208
Froehlich, Clifford P., 196

G

Glanz, Edward C., 83
Glick, S. J., 127
Griffin, Jack, 207
Group Guidance:
  approach and technique, 77, 79, 84–85
  basis for selecting members, 81, 86–87
  definition, 79–82
  group work, 80
  implementation of, 82
  leadership, 81, 86
  methods of disseminating information, 70–72
  principles involved, 86
  relationship to group counseling, 79–82
  size of group, 81
Guidance Program:
  allocation of authority, 189
  cooperation, 188
  defining working relationships, 199–200
  flexibility, importance of, 191
  in-service training, 193–194
  leadership, 188
  organization, 187–188
  patterns of organization, 191–193
  Presbyterian Guidance, 95–96
  problems, typical, 197–198
  public relations, 200
  research design, 176
  responsibility of administrators, 194
  responsibility of teachers, 195
  staff communication, 199
  statement of objectives, 188

Gutsch, K. U., 70, 88, 116, 145
Gutsch-Alcorn Test Scanner, 56–63

H

Hawes, G. R., 150
Hoppock, Robert, 75, 80, 82
Human Relationships:
  between counselor and teachers, 127–130
  between teacher and students, 128–133
  empathic, 128
  feelings of security, 128–129
  friendliness, 128–129
Hummel, Dean L., 184
Hutson, Percival W., 168

I

Impulsivity, 93–94
Individual inventory, 195
Information:
  classification of, 67–69
  dissemination, 70
  field visitation, 71, 72
  filmstrip, use of, 71
  group approach, use of, 71
  newspapers, use of, 70, 71
  Occupational Scanner, use of, 69, 70
  resource persons, use of, 72
  service, 67–77
  sources, 19
  techniques used to gain, 132
Information Service, 67
In-service training:
  teachers, 126, 193–194
Intake interview, 36
  importance of, 43
  personal data sheets, 36, 37, 38
  preliminary information, 36

Interviews, 19, 43
  employment, 160
  use in guidance research, 202–203

J

Jastak, J. F., 119
Jastak, S. R., 119
Jessner, Lucie, 125
Job Placement, 135–136, 138–139, 151, 155
  employment interview, 160
  initial contact, 159
  job application form, 156–157
  sample application letter, 161

K

Kaiser, H., 107
Kaplan, Louis, 118, 131
Knapp, R. H., 27, 130
Kroll, A. M., 170
Kuder Preference Record, 41, 42
  non-vocational interest, 41, 42
  readministered, 42
  vocational interest, 41, 42
Kvaraceus, W. C., 127

L

Laughlin, H. P., 109
Lighthall, Frederick F., 104
Logan, R. H. III, 70
Lovejoy, C. E., 150

M

May, R., 102
Morality:
  illustrations, 201–208

N

Nordberg, Robert B., 179, 182

O

Occupational literature:
  Dictionary of Occupational titles, 69
  free and inexpensive approach, 153–154
  general information file, 153
  selecting, 154
Occupational Scanner, 69, 70
Occupational Survey, 137
Organization:
  basic steps, 188
  flexibility, importance of, 191
  patterns of organization, 191–192
  problems, typical, 197–198
Orientation, 84
  precounseling, 95–96
  techniques, 84–85
Otto, Henry J., 187
Overholt, D. C., 151

P

Pace, C. R., 150
Permission for release of information:
  release form, 53
Personal Data Sheets, 36–38, 159
  sample, 159
Personality:
  characteristics, 42, 43
  illustrative story, 201–208
  inventories, 42
Personal rating, 22
Pierce, G. E., 162
Placement service, 135
  academic placement, 135–136

INDEX

Placement service (*Cont.*)
  bulletin, 155
  coordinating capacity of, 135, 141
  counseling, 136
  data processing, 162
  educational placement, 139
  file, 154
  job placement, 139–140, 151
  personal data, 158
  professional, 135
  team approach, 138
Preliminary information, 36

Q

Questionnaire, 21
  development of, 176–180
  example, 179–180
  occupational survey, 137
  personal data, 21
  use in program appraisal, 176

R

Rank, Otto, 123
Rautman, A. L., 206
Reading disability, 118–123
Reitz, Donald J., 179, 182
Reporting, 18, 30
  confidential report (example), 44–53
  cumulative record, 18, 30
  final, 44
  guidance reporting, 35
  profile summary, 48
Riccio, Anthony C., 169, 175
Roeber, Edward C., 188, 191
Rogers, Carl, 112

S

Sachs, Georgia M., 168

Separation anxiety:
  characteristics, 123–124
  traumatic effect, 123–124
Sex differences, 117–118
Shyness, 125–126
Smith, Glenn E., 178, 188, 191
Sociograms, 22
  defined, 22
  example, 22
SRA verbal and non-verbal tests, 39
  interpretations, 39–41
  use of, 39–53
Staffing, 38, 199
  principles of communication, 199–200
Steele, John E., 161
Stern, G. G., 150
Strang, Ruth, 19
Survey method:
  in program evaluation, 174

T

Test administration:
  administering and scoring, 26
  approach, 24
  caution, indiscriminate testing, 27, 28
  faculty involvement, 27
  grade level, 56–63
  importance of, 23
  selection and rationale, 24, 25, 56
Test evaluation:
  checklist, 22
  Gutsch-Alcorn Test Scanner (GATS), 56–63
  publishers, list of, 64–66
Testing:
  achievement, 40
  aptitude, 40, 41
  intelligence, 39, 40

Testing (*Cont.*)
  interest, 41, 42
  personality, 42, 43
Test interpretation, 27, 28, 29, 54
Torrance, E. Paul, 125

V

Visitation:
  in home, 23
  orientation technique, 84

Visual disorientation, 18, 118

W

Waldfogel, Samuel, 125
Willey, Roy D., 129
Wise, John E., 179, 182

Z

Zeran, Franklin R., 169, 175